CROSSING THE BORDER

CROSSING THE BORDER

Encounters between
Homeless People
and Outreach Workers

MICHAEL ROWE

University of California Press
Berkeley · Los Angeles · London

University of California Press
Berkeley and Los Angeles, California

University of California Press, Ltd.
London, England

© 1999 by the Regents of the University of California

Library of Congress Cataloging-in-Publication Data

Rowe, Michael
    Crossing the border : encounters between homeless people and
outreach workers / Michael Rowe.
        p.   cm.
    Includes bibliographical references and index.
    ISBN 0-520-21831-0 (alk. paper). —ISBN 0-520-21883-3
(alk. paper)
        1. Homeless persons—Services for—Connecticut—New Haven.
    2. Homeless persons—Mental health—Connecticut—New Haven.
    3. Homeless persons—Rehabilitation—Connecticut—New Haven.
    4. Marginality, Social—Connecticut—New Haven.   I. Title.
    HV4506.C8R68   1999
    362.5'8'097468—dc21   98-42986
                                                                                            CIP

Manufactured in the United States of America
08   07   06   05   04   03   02   01   00   99
10   9   8   7   6   5   4   3   2   1

The paper used in this publication meets the minimum
requirements of ANSI/NISO Z39.48-1992 (R 1997)
(*Permanence of Paper*). ♾

For my mother and in memory of my father

Contents

Preface

In January 1994, I began work as the director of an outreach project in New Haven, Connecticut. The project, called ACCESS (Access to Community Care and Effective Services and Supports), is one of eighteen in the country that are part of a national research demonstration to test the effectiveness of "systems integration" strategies for work with mentally ill homeless persons. The national project is under the direction of the federal Center for Mental Health Services; the New Haven project is a component of the Connecticut Mental Health Center, a public institution jointly operated by the Yale Department of Psychiatry and the state of Connecticut.

The practice of "assertive mental health outreach" to homeless persons was pioneered during the 1980s, but it was still new to many urban areas when the ACCESS demonstration began. There was an air of excitement and some trepidation among the emerging staff group that was being formed in New Haven. As an administrator with previous experience running social service programs and as a sociologist with some experience studying them, I thought that the project's success would depend in part on our developing an organizational fluidity and esprit de corps that are hard to achieve within large public bureaucracies. I was interested in the question of how or whether innovative programs that draw a good deal of their identity from their "newness" can survive, given that they face the twin dilemmas of being located within traditional service organizations and of suffering their own inevitable loss of zeal over time as work routines are put into place and client populations become better known.

It was a good question, I think. But the heart of the matter, I soon learned, was in the meetings that were already taking place on the streets between homeless persons and outreach workers. Organizational influences formed part of the context of outreach work, but it was the meetings themselves, I decided, that I ought to study. Over the next year and a half, and with continued learning and observation over the following three years, I learned about homeless individuals and outreach workers through the day-to-day work of managing the project, accompanying outreach workers on their rounds, standing in soup kitchen lines, and visiting emergency shelters. At other times I explored these same sites with a formerly homeless "guide." I also conducted seventy open-ended interviews with homeless people, outreach workers, and historians of homelessness in New Haven, supplementing them with informal observation and with participation in outreach team meetings.

Let me outline some characteristics of the homeless persons and outreach workers who agreed to talk with me. Of the fifty homeless persons I interviewed, forty-three were or became ACCESS clients, which means they had a mental illness as determined by an intake interview for the national outcome study, a study separate from my own. I asked ACCESS clinicians to give their own clinical impressions of the forty-three ACCESS clients. They rated nineteen, or about 40 percent, as having a psychotic or affective disorder (severe forms of mental illness), and twenty-six, or about 60 percent, as having a "co-occurring" substance abuse problem in addition to a mental illness. Of the remaining seven individuals (out of fifty), whom I met mostly through non-ACCESS case workers, at least two had been diagnosed with a mental illness and at least two others had histories of substance abuse.

Thirty-eight of the fifty individuals were male. Twenty-nine were white, eighteen were African American, and three were Hispanic. Forty of them were at least thirty years old, and about half of those were forty or older. Fourteen had been homeless for up to six months, ten for between six months and a year, and twenty-six for a year or more. Twelve identified themselves or were identified by clinicians as "street" homeless people, meaning they slept outside. Twenty-nine were "shelter users," and nine used both the streets and shelters. Thirty-two had lived within about twenty-five miles of New Haven for several years, and most of the thirty-two had grown up in New Haven or adjoining towns. At least eight of the thirty-eight males were veterans. About two-thirds of the group of fifty had worked more than an odd day of temporary labor here and there. Some criminal history was common among clients of the ACCESS project, usually in the form of drug charges (including selling prescription drugs), charges of writing bad checks, or convictions for breach of the peace. At least a dozen of the people I interviewed had significant medical problems aside from mental illness. Injuries sustained on the job or medical conditions such as arthritis or a bad back sometimes barred people from work they had done in the past. Some clients of the outreach project were infected with HIV, but I do not have figures for my cohort.

To make contacts for interviews, I used outreach and shelter staff, former homeless persons, and people I met while doing my field work. I obtained written consent and did not pay people, although I did buy coffee and food when the opportunity presented itself. With one exception—a phone interview—I audiotaped interviews at two local shelters, at my office, and at a Burger King in the New Haven Mall.

I also interviewed fifteen outreach workers. I use the term *outreach workers* generically for workers whose training spans a number of degrees and disciplines. My staff cohort included a psychiatrist, social workers, a physician assistant, nurses, individuals with undergraduate degrees, and others, including two formerly homeless persons, with high school educations. New Haven ACCESS, although a project of the Connecticut Mental Health Center, is an interagency effort as well as an interdisciplinary one. Staff represent the mental health center, an emergency shelter, a community health center, a residential agency for chronic mental patients, and a vocational rehabilitation agency. Eight of the fifteen staff were female. Eight were white, four were African American, two were Hispanic, and one was Surinamese. They ranged in age from mid-twenties to late forties. I audiotaped these interviews as well, usually in my office. I should also note that I use pseudonyms for both homeless persons and outreach workers throughout this book.

A few caveats are in order. My study was limited by time and place and by the characteristics of the people I interviewed. My research setting was an aging, midsize industrial city in the Northeast. Had my setting been a large city, the homeless terrain would have looked different. Had I conducted my research two years later, I would have met more women who were homeless, not as single persons, but with their children, and I would have talked to individuals within an emerging context of managed health care and welfare reform. In addition, almost all of the homeless persons I interviewed had been diagnosed with a mental illness or substance abuse or both. Recent scholarly estimates of the incidence of serious mental illness among homeless persons range from a third down to about a fifth.[1] Substance abuse among the homeless has been estimated at about one-third,[2] and the incidence of co-occurring mental illness and substance abuse at between 10 and 20 percent (a wide range, to be sure).[3] Numerous as each of these subgroups may be, they do not represent the homeless population in general. Thus I make no claim to have studied a representative sample of the single adult homeless population.

As for the staff members I interviewed, they would have been more streetwise and seasoned in the ways of outreach had I conducted my research at a later point, but they might also have been less spontaneous in talking about their explorations in homeless territory. The locus of my research was a homeless outreach team hosted by a large public mental health center. Had the host organization been a smaller nonprofit agency, the internal temperature generated in the outreach worker by the friction between individual care and institutional people-processing might have dropped a few degrees. But only a few, perhaps: the non-profit agency would have been receiving government funds. It would have been located within a social service "system." And outreach workers would still have been subject to administrative regulations and been obliged to help their clients maneuver through other social service organizations with categorical program requirements.

In the end, this is an exploratory, hypothesis-generating study, with the potential strength of pointing to new areas for investigation and the potential deficit of small numbers and a lack of empirical proof that such studies often have. My aim is to contribute to our understanding of the meetings between homeless persons and outreach workers, and of our relationship to all those persons, homeless or not, who cling to or stand outside our cultural and social borders.

I am fortunate to have had the opportunity to participate in the national ACCESS research demonstration as the project director of a local ACCESS site. I also want to thank a number of people who helped me complete this study. They are the homeless persons, outreach workers, and homeless advocates and agency staff who agreed to talk to me. They are Michael Hoge, Debbie Fisk, and Dori Laub, with whom I have written papers about homelessness that enrich this report;[4] Paul Johnston, who taught me about the study of the city; and Dorrie McMonigal, who transcribed over seventy interviews. They are Jim Baumohl and Rob Rosenthal, who each gave me detailed and insightful comments on an earlier draft of this book. Naomi Schneider, my editor at the University of California Press, has seen this manuscript through several "final" versions with good humor and steady support, and I appreciate her faith in this project. Kai Erikson's guidance and friendship, as well as the inspiration of his work and his painstaking critiques of mine, have been a privilege for me. I owe a special debt of gratitude to him. Finally, I want to thank my wife, Gail, who stood by my side, who cheered me on, and who waited patiently.

I

Introduction

Homeless encounters, in this book, involve face-to-face meetings between people who are homeless and the rescuers, called outreach workers, whom society dispatches to its margins. These encounters are composed of mutual perceptions, negotiated understandings about behavior and identity, and the transfer of goods. I refer to these encounters as "homeless" not only because homeless persons are a party to them, but also because they lack a foothold in everyday social interactions or in the office-bound meetings of clients and workers. Different images and expectations adhere to them, and the actors are playing for higher stakes. Homeless encounters take place at a border that divides one world from another. This border is physical, in the sense that it is staked out by emergency shelters, soup kitchens, and the streets, and it is social and psychological, in the sense that it is staked out by experiences and perceptions. For each party, the act of crossing the border is physical, social, and psychological, a movement of identity as well as of place.

By the "margins," I mean the edges of the established social order where instability of housing and social support and the experience of severe poverty put individuals at a high risk of becoming homeless. The margins have also been identified as "endangered spaces on the civic landscape that supplied forgiving accommodations to misfits of all sorts, at a cost conventionally figured in disgrace rather than dollars."[1] The disappearance of skid rows and other such forgiving accommodations for those who cannot or will not pursue the American dream renders many such individuals dependent on help from the government and social service programs. Keeping in mind both definitions, and adding the assumption that margins of the latter sort still provide some pockets of accommodation, we can see that workers, by moving homeless individuals out of their current marginal niches, may give with one hand and take away with the other. This report starts from the premise that the symbolic and practical aspects of homeless (or boundary) encounters are intertwined. Negotiations over the instrumental pathways to housing are shaped by negotiations over what the homeless person's housed identity will be. Outreach workers distribute tangible goods, but feel that they must also make contact with a core sense of self in homeless persons in order to help them make successful border crossings. Now, to talk about borders and crossings is to say there is a line to cross and that homeless persons and outreach workers stand on either side of it. There are problems with that image. For one thing, it can encourage a colonial fallacy that all those on the other side want to be on ours.[2] For another, it can encourage a static conception of homelessness, when the fact is that many individuals shuttle back and forth between being without homes and being barely housed, staying briefly with friends or family or securing their own place, then going back to the streets when they lose their income or overtax the resources of their intimates.[3] And finally, it can reinforce the stereotype of wholly "other" persons who inhabit a savage frontier, much as ethnic stereotypes, characterized by exaggeration and selective perception, set up the terms for crossing an imaginary boundary and persist even in the face of observed traffic back and forth.[4] The danger of stereotyping is even more acute when the "others," like the homeless persons described in this book, carry the added stigma of mental illness.

The notion of a line to be crossed, then, can both sharpen and obscure our vision. For our purposes, *border* will refer in part to the point at which mainstream society loses its hold and in part to perceptions of borders and the routes by which perception becomes reality. Taken together, the notions of borders and border crossings will concern the ways in which we respond not only to the needs of homeless persons but also, through the lens of homeless encounters, to "the needs of strangers"[5] of all categorical stripes. These encounters do not stand alone. They require homeless individuals to be rescued and outreach workers to be dispatched by human service organizations. Their meaning will be distorted if we overlook the bureaucratic pathways that lead to them, and they will lack substance if we fail to consider both homeless persons' experience of homelessness and the seductions and dangers that come for outreach workers who wander far from the centers of institutional life.

Homeless persons have an odd identity thrust upon them. Their status is an antistatus and their careers as homeless persons are noncareers. A potential new identity as housed persons is part of what they negotiate in their encounters with outreach workers. They contemplate the worker's offer of tangible services and help in finding a new identity, and they weigh this package against the reality of giving up the difficult but known life of homelessness. The prospect of crossing the border may arouse deep fears in them. They may balk at giving up their freedom and taking on the responsibilities that come with having a home. They may realize that shedding their negative public identity as homeless persons gives them no guarantee of openings in the mainstream identity pool.

Outreach workers look two ways as well. They are simultaneously client advocates and gatekeepers who operate under the aegis of institutional rules and processes. They see damaged lives and deep social needs. They also see bureaucratic requirements that undermine individual care. In trying to juggle contradictory demands, they confront the possibility that they will not be able to deliver the goods they have promised. They are susceptible to the fears about homeless persons that most of us share and, at the same time, to a complementary temptation to plunge into the mystery of life at the margins.

The meetings of homeless people and outreach workers can be seen as the center of a web laid across a symbolic and physical border separating the two parties. Homeless persons are the filaments that radiate toward the center from their side of the border. The filaments that cross them are their family and work histories, their disabilities and vulnerabilities, the shelters, soup kitchens, and other sites where they spend their days, and the social and economic conditions that affect them. Outreach workers are the filaments that radiate toward the center of the web from their side of the border. The filaments that cross them are their cultural and professional associations, the resources they bring to their work, and the institutional requirements that dictate how much help they can give and to whom.

The "homelessness," or lack of structure, of boundary encounters suggests the possibility of transformation on both sides, even of partnerships to advocate for social change. There is also danger in the margins, as Mary Douglas has written. Here, the structure of ideas that shapes and guides a society breaks down.[6] Values that we see as timeless and universal when we stand near the center may be seen as tangled up with power and self-interest when we stand at the edge. The gaze of Reason herself, studied from afar, may appear not as disinterested, as turned away from common pursuits, but as focused—as "a look of concentration, a look of one who is privately engaged in a difficult, treacherous task,"[7] that of defending her vast empire. We may guess that society will protect itself from the trauma of knowing this traumatized group at its margins and that the disruptive implications of outreach work will be contained, either by watering down the knowledge such work uncovers or by keeping that knowledge at bay. Services and tangible resources together are the mediating factors that contain this knowledge for outreach workers and shield them from a moral terror that may come from their exposure to the alien culture of homelessness. Together, they are a tool both for making contact with homeless persons and for containing the possibilities generated by such contacts.

The mediating quality of services leads us from the homelessness of meetings at the edge to social and organizational elements of status, function, and power. Meetings between workers and clients involve negotiations over identity and the terms of success, but the actors have unequal power. There are people who can dispense services and people who can accept them. Now, to speak of social negotiations and the price of obtaining services is not to minimize the disabilities of many homeless individuals or the deprivations of life on the street. Providing clinical care to severely mentally ill persons, in some cases even coercively, may show greater respect for their dignity than simply leaving them alone for fear of violating their privacy.[8] But this point does not resolve the tension of the encounter between the helper and the helped, and it does not reduce the high stakes for which the latter is playing. Can the outreach worker make an offer that does not force the homeless person to accept the identity of patient or client?

This question prompts another. How do homeless persons view outreach workers? They may see them as allies or as representatives of people-processing systems. Outreach work is a kind of advocacy, but an advocacy that must be held in check by the institutions that sponsor the work. Even the nature of time shifts between the institution and the street, from regulated to contingent and from scheduled to improvisational.[9] Do workers carry organizational time into the field? And when they do, is it interpreted by potential clients as an attempt to seize control over one of the few resources available to them—their time? Are workers primarily agents of the state who offer homeless people a ticket to second-class citizenship in exchange for a loss of freedom?

Citizenship, in this report, involves the strength and form of the individual's connection to the rights, responsibilities, and resources that society offers to people through public and social institutions. In Paul Johnston's terms, a critical distinction between full citizenship and "clienthood" is whether individuals can demand satisfaction from public institutions or have to take what they can get from them, whether they are consumers and thus subjects in relation to these institutions, or clients and thus objects of them.[10] For this study, I will define three rough levels of citizenship: full citizenship, with strong practical and psychological connections to mainstream institutions, rights, and responsibilities; second-class citizenship, with marginal connections to these institutions, rights, and responsibilities; and noncitizenship, in which the individual is severed from society. Outreach workers cannot bequeath full citizenship, but they can provide services that may place individuals at the second level. Whether workers can do more than the latter, if somewhat less than the former, is a question I will consider in this study.

Boundary encounters contain implicit questions not only about the efforts we should make to help people at the margins but also about where those efforts should stop. What social obligation do we have to the disenfranchised? What level of enfranchisement should we ask them to accept, and what mainstream responses of work, gratitude, and behavior should we expect them to give? Beyond the interpersonal encounter and the individual outcome, these are questions that we ask when we send our representatives to the margins. The results of these encounters, on a large scale, are a measure of where we will set our social boundary and of what standard of living we will accept for those who live at that boundary.

A study such as this one requires that the researcher encounter homelessness too. For me, this happened through my work as director of the New Haven ACCESS outreach project. My encounter with homelessness was akin to that of outreach workers, since I wore the hat of program official and had the power to dispense help. As a researcher, though, I had the additional responsibility of searching for intangible themes that weave through the administration of services. My position gave me an entree to the subjects of my study, but it carried with it a potential loss of objectivity, since I had a manager's investment in his clients' and program's success. In addition, one could argue that homeless individuals and outreach workers would have reasons to please me and thus might feed me "tainted" data. Against these possible objections I would offer a few considerations. First, as a non-clinician (a sociologist) in a mental health outreach program, I had something of an outsider's status for reflecting on the work. Second, many homeless persons whom I encountered in the field (as opposed to those I formally interviewed) did not know me. Third, while I was self-conscious about my influence as an authority figure, my impression was that homeless individuals and outreach workers were as likely to open up to me because I understood their concerns as they were to skew their observations because of my position.

Finally, the open-ended interviews I conducted with both parties did not point to any obviously right or wrong answers. With homeless persons, my questions were broad at the outset: I asked people what caused them to be homeless, what homelessness was like for them, and what they thought of outreach workers. These questions were opening points for discussions that could range as wide and as deep as people were willing to go with them. (And I was often surprised at how far they were willing to go. Does the omnipresence of technology in the form of the tape recorder unite us in an American fantasy of having our fifteen minutes of fame? Does the tape recorder prompt our need to tell our story to an unseen but hoped-for audience? Each of these is part of it, I think, but I imagine that the experience of being tape-recorded also allows us, for a moment, to transform ourselves and our relationship to others, to feel a thrill of recognition and an odd, disquieting wave of freedom as we "hear" others listen to our story in another time and another place.) My interviews with staff were also open-ended but oriented toward broad concerns such as their perceptions of the causes of homelessness and their strategies for approaching homeless individuals and assessing their needs.

Given the open-ended nature of my interviews, then, it

seemed to me that, with a few exceptions, it would have been difficult for either group to know how to please me. One exception involved my questions to homeless persons about outreach workers. Individuals who were negotiating for services might be expected to extol the virtues of workers with whom I was associated. This did happen, but just as often people complained to me about delays in getting help. The latter response could be tainted as well: was my subject truly frustrated or just pushing buttons to get me to speed things up? In the end, participant-observers must sift through their own and others' motivations for signs that can keep them on track or derail them.

At times, I was recognized in the field as a staff person when I was not actively assuming that role. If a question about my program role came up or was implied, I said I was the director. When I interviewed homeless individuals whom I had not met through outreach workers, I explained that I worked with the outreach project and was trying to learn more about homelessness in order to help improve programs and educate the public. If the conversation seemed to call for it, I gave my title.

I used the tools of an outreach worker to further my learning as a researcher. Mentioning the outreach project could be the opening I needed for conversations with homeless individuals who might not have talked to me as a researcher. Decisions to use such program tools are not always pure or disinterested. I entered a zone of discomfort when I went into the field. I might walk a gauntlet of homeless persons in a local emergency shelter. Along the hall that divides this former convent in half, people talk to each other, ignore or study the passersby, or keep their eyes glued to the floor. In the lounge, people watch TV, all facing the same way. In the dining room, people are congregated in lively or sullen groups, neither of which are recruiting new members. And in any case I am not here to eat, even if I do. I am hanging out not for its own sake but because I want information. I am not shelter staff and I am not a homeless "guest." I feel physically safe but morally and culturally unsafe. Having access to the tools of the staff person, I may feel inclined to use them for other than the dispassionate concerns of science.

My dual role as researcher and program official could make for awkward encounters. Let me give an example. Miss Lil, an African American woman of about fifty, lived in a house made of cardboard cartons and plywood scraps and kept her belongings in a shopping cart. She was known to distrust people who were associated with the public mental health center, so I was surprised when she agreed to meet me at a local Wendy's. We sat in a booth with Linda, the outreach worker who had arranged the meeting. Miss Lil eyed my tape recorder suspiciously. I offered to take notes instead. In her soft, almost inaudible voice, she berated the Wendy's manager who had yelled at her for knocking over a Wet Floor sign. My beeper went off. I cursed silently and went across the street to look for a pay phone, in full view of Miss Lil through the plate-glass window. For the next ten minutes I walked up and down the street, finally locating a phone outside an auto-parts store right across the street from Wendy's. It was my boss at the mental health center.

When I came back, Linda said Miss Lil wasn't ready to be interviewed today. Perhaps another time. Miss Lil looked across the restaurant at the Wendy's manager. She said there was nothing she wanted from him that he could give her. She paid for what she got. Her implied question to me was clear: "What do you have that I need? And what do I have to pay for it?" She turned to Linda, smiled, and said, "You're persistent." There were four of us at the table: Miss Lil, Linda, the manager (symbolically), and me. Would I, too, be persistent in my concern, or was I out to use her like others?

Perhaps the outcome of this meeting would have been the same had my beeper not interrupted us, but for me the encounter was an object lesson in the difficulty of disentangling my research and program roles in the field.

Participant-observers must weigh their own culture shock against what is happening around them. One evening I stood in a soup kitchen line at a downtown church. People seemed drawn into themselves and mostly did not speak to each other. A woman came out from the kitchen and welcomed us. One of the patrons said a prayer. There were smiling faces at the serving table, but the long line curving around at the perimeter of the community room cast a pall over this ritual, and the instructions about second helpings added to the Depression-era gloom. I sat at a table with three other men and made a lame attempt at conversation. One of my companions answered politely and then ignored me. I picked at the spaghetti, ate a cookie, and went upstairs. Sometime later I visited the church again on a soup kitchen night. It was a noisy, jarring scene, full of poor people worrying about welfare cuts, but it lacked the sense of quiet gloom of my earlier visit. Was the gloom of the first night my response to a confrontation with deep poverty? Or was I now hardened to such scenes and blind to a substratum of despair sitting heavily beneath the bustle of the second night? Participant-observers must keep their eyes and ears open to their environment and to what stirs within them, even when they cannot give sure answers to their own questions.

Participant-observers must study their inner turmoil as well as the encounters that arouse it.[11] During one interview, a homeless addict, after telling me about the con games he used to feed his addiction, alluded to other, "humanly nasty" things he had done to stay high and survive on the streets. I was disgusted, more by the unspoken secrets I imagined him to be concealing than by the con games he recounted. He said we should have compassion for evil people. I guessed that he was either trying to come to terms with his own evil or playing me for compassion. The whiff of evil and the shame of being manipulated fueled my revulsion. I wanted to con the con man: *You know every game in the book?* I silently asked, wearing a mask of concern. *Well, here's a game I can win. I can make you target population or I can break you. I can wave the goodies under your nose and walk away and you'll never know what you could have had.*

The point of including this story is not to confess my own sins, but to say that the researcher who adopts ethnographic methods moves through successive levels of comfort and discomfort that simultaneously give clues to and reflect his penetration of the alien culture. His revelations and discomforts are doors that open into the objects of his study and into himself. The ethnographer, as Paul Rabinow suggests, uses his cultural moorings to understand his deep allegiance with and yet final difference from the "other."[12] His appreciation of his own otherness and of the other's sameness with himself allows him to cross borders of meaning while acknowledging that there is a border of difference he cannot cross.

The remainder of this study is divided into five chapters. In chapter 2, I attempt to draw a collective (and partial) portrait of the homeless persons I interviewed and observed, focusing on the themes of contingency, negativity, and perceived incompetence. In chapter 3, I discuss outreach workers, including the founding principles and ethos of their work, their perceptions of homeless persons, and their methods of identifying and approaching potential clients.

In chapter 4, I examine boundary transactions from the perspective of each party, and the price of help for the homeless individual who faces an uncertain future in mainstream society. In chapter 5, I place boundary encounters within their institutional context by examining the opposing goals of individual care and institutional people-processing with which workers must contend. I review strategies that workers and teams develop to maintain their effectiveness and consider the alternate prospects of "program" and "full" citizenship for homeless persons who accept services from outreach workers. And in the concluding chapter, I summarize and expand upon certain themes considered earlier.

2

Homeless People

New Haven, host to the encounters of this report, can be described as an aging manufacturing town that has not made a comfortable transition to a service economy. Like many other cities in the Northeast, it has suffered from economic downturns, with industry moving out, the local economy stagnating, and the city government strapped for cash.[1] In 1960, one in four jobs in the city were manual labor jobs; in 1992, that figure was one in ten.[2] Businesses were offered generous tax subsidies to reverse these trends. This policy merely reduced the city's potential tax base and increased the tax burden on homeowners, while businesses continued to leave town.[3] A dual exodus of the white middle class and retail businesses to the suburbs during this period also contributed to the city's economic decline.[4]

New Haven is a city of contrasts, home to deep poverty and social problems on one hand, and to Yale University, one of the country's top research institutions, on the other. A tense town-gown relationship rumbles periodically along several fault lines. It can be seen in periodic labor disputes with Yale, the city's largest employer, or in the occasional homeless person sleeping on the steps of one of the Yale secret society buildings. Still, although New Haven's reputation and economic well-being have suffered because of crime and violence, Yale's intellectual and cultural capital lends New Haven a cosmopolitan air unusual for a city of 120,000. New Haven is solidly Democratic and is unusually rich in social service programs, even if services are uncoordinated and sometimes work at cross-purposes.

New Haven, like other American cities, has been vulnerable to national trends that set the stage for widespread contemporary homelessness. Starting in the 1950s, thousands of flophouses and single room occupancy buildings (SROs)—housing options of last resort for many marginal persons—were condemned and torn down in cities across the country for more profitable urban uses such as middle-class dwellings.[5] With a seller's market and a decline in public assistance housing, poor people increasingly had to compete with the middle class for a scarce supply of dwelling space.[6] In the early 1980s, housing vacancy rates in urban areas were as low as 1 to 2 percent. By 1986, 6 million households spent more than 50 percent of their income on housing.[7] The number of poor households increased, and poor families had fewer resources to support their dependents, especially those with disabilities.[8] Poor families doubled up in housing with their poor relatives. The next stop for many of these "houseless" families was literal homelessness.

During those decades the economic base of the American city was undergoing a radical transformation from a manufacturing to a service economy. Unskilled or semiskilled workers lost their jobs as industry left cities,[9] and the unskilled work that was available paid a low wage.[10] During the late 1970s and the 1980s, changes in income support benefits also put many poor people at risk of becoming homeless. Supplemental Security Income (SSI), a Social Security program for persons with mental or physical disabilities, lost "real value" due to inflation, while eligibility requirements were tightened and many individuals were denied benefits. Cuts in other welfare programs such as local General Assistance (GA) and federal-state Aid to Families with Dependent Children (AFDC) also pushed vulnerable individuals to the brink of homelessness.[11] Economic and political forces in tandem lowered "the threshold at which personal impairment becomes social handicap."[12] Thus, mental illness and substance abuse increased one's vulnerability to becoming homeless.

Mirroring a national trend, homeless persons began to appear on the streets of New Haven in the late 1970s and early 1980s. By 1985, Columbus House, New Haven's first emergency shelter for singles, was turning away more than fifty people each night. When a subsidized public housing project was closed the following year, nine hundred inner-city families became homeless or were moved into "temporary" slum dwellings with high rates of drug abuse and crime. A tent city on the Green organized by homeless advocates and church groups helped to raise public awareness of homelessness and put pressure on the city to take action.

Over the next few years, the city of New Haven funded shelter beds and adopted an ambitious homeless plan that included housing with social service support for all homeless persons and special programs for women and substance abusers. By the fall of 1990, though, the city's ability to provide operating funds for this plan was in doubt (according to city officials) because of the cost of complying with a court order to provide shelter on demand.[13] Federal research funds paid for a shelter and treatment program for homeless male substance abusers, but by the early 1990s public concern about homelessness had waned and the city's homeless plan was a dead letter. City officials blamed fiscal problems and the court order (which was later set aside). Many service providers and advocates for homeless persons blamed the administration of John Daniels, the mayor at that time, for inaction and lack of commitment to the problem.

In 1993, as federal funding for homeless male substance abusers ended, funding for the New Haven ACCESS project was secured for outreach work with mentally ill homeless persons. As I noted before, most of the homeless individuals I interviewed were or became ACCESS clients. The crisscrossing filaments of these individuals' lives prior to meeting outreach workers could fill a volume much thicker than this one. In this chapter, I will concentrate on those filaments that spun around the interrelated and overlapping themes of contingency, negativity, and perceived incompetence. These themes seem to me particularly important for the emotional valence they lend to these individuals' encounters with outreach workers.

CONTINGENCY

Contingency implies adjustment to, and thus a measure of control over, outside forces and events whose general direction we cannot change. Many homeless individuals are geniuses of contingency, mixing and matching scant resources and changing strategies at the dictates of chance.[14] The orderly sequence of events and orientation toward future goals characteristic of mainstream time gives way to the skilled use of timing on the streets: when to act in order to produce the best possible effect and then move on.[15] Conversations, chance meetings, immediate survival strategies, and tricks to combat boredom are key temporal points. Any choice can be replaced by another opportunity, and opportunity has a short half-life on the street. A small moment for you and me—whether to greet an acquaintance we should make contact with but would just as soon not—may be a crucial moment in the calculus of the homeless person's day. His choice can lead him in the direction of a night's shelter or mean a missed opportunity to catch the busy outreach worker who might help him get an apartment. This contingent sense of time is indispensable for survival on the streets, but it is ill adapted to social service bureaucracies that slot predictable activities for clients and staff.[16]

People who are homeless face a day-to-day struggle to survive, and constant struggle wears people down. Rob Rosenthal has observed that people who expend their energy gathering resources for survival have little energy left to gather more substantial resources for their exit from homelessness. Lack of positive contact with mainstream society both reflects and exacerbates this dilemma. The will to escape homelessness and the ability to gather the necessary resources begin to erode, whittling each other down as the length of time one spends without a home increases and escape becomes increasingly unlikely.[17] Contingency carries with it a sense of living on the pulse of the moment, but constant contingency can be as boring as it is uncertain. The following is a composite list of some key points around which many of the people I talked to built their day: Get up at around six if you're staying in the shelter (earlier if you're sleeping under a bridge or selling newspapers). Leave the shelter by half past seven. Have breakfast at the soup kitchen "if they're giving out anything edible." Go down the block and get some day labor if you're up to it, or go to the Burger King for coffee if you have the eighty-nine cents, or to the Copper Kitchen restaurant if you're really flush. Kill time. Hang out on the Green and wait for the library to open or get warm at the Mall until they kick you out. Sit and read in the library if it's open or go to City Welfare if you have an appointment. Go to the drop-in center and watch TV. Kill time. Go to the soup kitchen for lunch or skip it if it interferes with scraping money together by panhandling, collecting cans, selling newspapers, or getting day labor. Get high if you get high, buy a bottle and drink with your buddies if that's what you do, or just kill time straight. If you can juggle the contradictions of homeless time and future plans, you might be able to put a little money away for an apartment. If you hope to sleep at one particular shelter that has limited beds for nonregulars, head back there to get in line and wait, good weather or bad. If you're not staying in the shelter, you may have a little more time to hang out.

Time, instead of being a tool for productive activity, becomes something you kill, over and over again, from one day to the next. Time has been described as a form of power. The more "free" time you have, the less power and the less integration into modern society. Homeless people spend much of their time waiting: for libraries to open, in lines at soup kitchens, in chairs at welfare departments. Waiting reinforces the homeless person's recognition of his powerlessness.[18] George Orwell put it this way: "The great redeeming feature of poverty" is that "it annihilates the future."[19] A bleak redemption! Homelessness is a contingent and lonely experience; it can also be physically dangerous, especially for those living on the streets. Homeless women fear sexual assault and other abuse from "hard-core" elements. "There's certain streets you don't walk down at night," said one woman, "certain people you don't mess with. You find another person who you walk with." Another woman learned to "be more aggressive and talk fast and be kind of curt." Men feared violence too. "You can't let them know you're prey," said one of street people, whom he saw as being "recycled" from the jails.

Friendship becomes a form of self-protection.[20] Mutual obligation and its companion, minding your own business, are twin rules of the road. Watch your friend's back and never turn yours. Like all rules of thumb, these are not infallible:

> People that are out on the street protect each other. It's a code of "You don't tell somebody's business, you don't get in other people's business, and I don't want to know their business." They will stand up for each other but in a split second they'll turn on each other.[21]

Kidd, a young African American male whom we will hear from again, said: "Sometimes you live in packs, sometimes you don't. You've got to trust somebody to watch your back." Still, while friends can help you stay alive on the streets, the bottom line for most is: "Everybody is trying to make it. Everybody trying to survive themselves."

In the shelters, keeping to yourself can be self-protection against a different kind of danger, that of blowing what you've got coming to you from cultivating the good graces of a shelter case manager. Keeping to yourself can be a personal style or a sign of withdrawal, especially for those with a mental illness. And keeping to yourself can stem from the recognition that there are always people waiting to take advantage of you. The social fence that many homeless persons set up around themselves is not merely a passive withdrawal into self. It is also a message to the sharks:

> You can't let your guard down. Once you let your guard down you're going to get suckered in. Borrowing money . . . they got a million ways they're going to pay you back but it just never happens.

Contingency implies a quality of drifting, sometimes from place to place in New Haven and sometimes from city to city. Frank, a white male, is a veteran drifter. The following exchange took place as I was trying to follow his itinerary from the point when he decided to leave Boston after going there from Portland, Maine:

> I left because I already stayed for three months—I stayed in one job for about a month but it took me two months to find a job. Now I'm in New Haven. I've been here for a couple of weeks.

Q. What made you decide to come to New Haven from Boston?
A. It was just the next city on the road after Providence. I stopped at Milford [a Connecticut town] for a while. Their shelter was closed so I took a train here and applied for jobs. I'm not sure where I'm going to stop. They offered housing but I haven't applied for it yet 'cause I haven't taken a steady job.

Q. Did you grow up in Portland?
A. No, I didn't. I grew up in Miami, Florida.

Q. How did you end up coming up here from Florida?
A. I drove my car and I wasn't sure where to go so I stopped in Maine. That was the last state up [before] Canada. I decided to stop in the largest city, which is Portland. I was able to stay at their shelter. I was working in a factory for a year. I wasn't sure about the cost of living there so I decided to leave the area.

There is another side to this seemingly footloose experience of homelessness, as Frank had learned:

> It's a slowly losing war. It's like climbing a mountain of snow with street shoes. You climb ten feet, you fall seven, you never gain any ground. You're always a little short. Everybody's in the same shape. Your friends are getting benefits and they can't help you or they screw up their benefits. You need an address for a homeless benefit, but how can you have an address if you're homeless? My friend let me use her address, but I can't stay with her. You get a couple of weeks' work, pay a couple of bills, you get shut off from all these systems. You don't have a phone for employers to call you, nobody wants to hire you if you're homeless. You just slowly sink. Nobody cares. You're broke, you're hungry, you're a burden. You don't want to bother your relatives, but who else are you going to bother? And they don't have it themselves.

Frank spoke to me over the phone because we were unable to agree on a time or place to meet. He talked further about the difficulty of finding work:

> You never get enough work or steady work, or the work pays so little. This happens, that happens, there are constant problems. You run out of gas, your car breaks down, you can't get to an interview. How can you survive in this economy? How can you live on five dollars an hour and pay your rent, your car insurance? You either do without or you don't do at all. The less you do, the less opportunities, the less chance you have of getting back on your feet.

Frank's life seems to be an object lesson in David Snow and Leon Anderson's "bad luck" theory that social and individual factors interact to make people homeless.[22] The oft-heard remark that most of us are only a paycheck or two away from becoming homeless is inaccurate. Most of us are a paycheck or two, plus loans from family and friends, plus a series of lower-paying jobs, away from becoming homeless. We are depleted bank accounts and credit lines and then the knowledge of how to negotiate service systems away from becoming homeless. We are a move to a cheaper apartment and then a doubling up with relatives away from becoming homeless. Finally, we are the blessing of not having a severe disability such as mental illness, substance abuse, or a physical handicap away from becoming homeless. In most cases the homeless person first had a career as a poor person. Additional problems such as the loss of social or economic reserves pushed him "over the edge."[23] The bad luck that hovers around all of us, then, sticks to those at the margins who lack the buffers with which those nearer the center are equipped. Homelessness is often the individual's last stop on a slow train of crises, bad luck, missed chances, and loss of support from family, friends, and institutions.[24]

Frank described the effect of contingency in his life:

> I've been an apartment manager here in Connecticut. I got an electrical license but I can't get any work. I was going to a friend's house, I got mugged. I had this swelling on my head, now I can't hear right. The welfare medical system won't find anything because they don't want to operate on you. I can't go to the homeless shelters because I had to evict some of them when I was an apartment manager. They could knife you in the back. So I stayed in my car. My car got smashed up by a girl on welfare with no insurance. It screwed up my back. I called the police. They took a report over the phone and then they couldn't find it when I needed it. A lawyer won't take the case because there's not enough money involved. I got a room because they said it was going to snow. My friend here is letting me use his phone.

This sense of drifting or falling from one event into another, of slipping on a banana peel and falling off a cliff, does capture an element of homeless life for many. But it may mystify as well. Contingency is not simply an attribute of marginal individuals who happened to fall on hard times or of a chaotic and dangerous life on the streets. A contingent way of life may begin long before the individual's first episode of homelessness. For the people I talked to, key past associations were family, work and money, and drugs.

FAMILY

A few individuals had drifted back and forth, in and out of state, from relative to relative. One man had been raised by his grand-mother, who went into a nursing home. He came north from Alabama to find that his parents had died of AIDS. He was "hanging out with some friends who decided to come to New Haven." He "had nothing to lose," so he came to New Haven with them and ended up in an emergency shelter. For another man, named Peter, the drifting impulse was connected to family as well:

> I was working fifty, sixty hours a week for this guy. It was pretty good and I saved a lot of money. It's getting near November, I was thinking about going to Florida to see my mom and my sisters for Thanksgivin'. The next morning I got on the bus and I went to Florida. I got all the ways to Florida and I hopped on the bus [and] came back 'cause I couldn't find them. I stopped in Virginia, I stayed the night. Next mornin' I said, "Fuck it, I'm going back to Florida." And I went to Florida and I took a taxi. They brought me right to where the hell it was and I just stayed there for thirteen months.

People looked back to a less marginal way of life or to one they could point to as setting them on their current path. There were the death of both parents,[25] arguments over inheritance, divorces, adoptions, foster care, and family alcoholism and drug addiction. In some cases both parents were dead, although the individual's contact with them may have been sporadic while they were alive. In others, individuals' family relationships were marginal prior to their becoming homeless. They had little hope of rebuilding them:

> I have family but I don't know where they are. They don't want to know me 'cause when my mom died . . . they haven't talked to me since '89.

> I have brothers but I don't know where they are. My mother's been dead for nine years. My father's been dead almost eighteen.

The cause of separation may be a tangled skein, but sometimes one event can be plucked out to stand for all. The bitterness of a homeless man's mother at his father's funeral, for example: his parents were long divorced and he had taken care of his father, a veteran. He was given an American flag at the cemetery and his mother never forgave him for taking what she thought was rightfully hers to reject.

A few individuals grew up with foster parents and gave the impression of having felt like "extra" people, burdens on their caretakers. Daniel, an African American in his early thirties, was taken from his mother when he was three and, from what staff could determine from his medical records and contacts with people who knew him, never met his father. He has foster family, whom he refers to as blood relatives, in the area, but they have others to care for, and no doubt his drug use and arrests strained their patience with him. The businessman in the following passage is Daniel's dream uncle who is also his dream brother. Daniel also refers to what was apparently an imaginary conversation with his father. Still, for all that his comments here are laced with his delusions, he describes a feeling of rejection and a need to keep one's distance from family that others share:

> He's got a roofing company. He's wealthy. If anybody in his peer group would see that I have anything to do with him, that would endanger his business. They would try to interfere with what he worked and strived and broke his back for. "Oh, that's your nephew out there. Why don't you help him out? Why don't you give him a place to stay?" If I were to go home it would create a problem. My family, both sides of my family, they said it: I'm the black sheep of the family. Not saying they don't love me, but even my father, he said he loved me but he just couldn't keep me.

The next passage provides clinicians with further evidence of Daniel's psychosis, since his reference point is a recent blood transfusion, but it also reflects his radical separation from family and friends:

> I had the same body but my blood and everything has been changed. I remember, I still remember, but the places I once was

at, I can't go there. I'm forbidden. People I used to stay with, homes I used to live in, I just can't go back to them. There's still a chair, still a window, still a bed, still a house, still a moon. The people still exist but I have no right to go there. I still know the people I knew before, but I'm farther away from them. I'm letting them go.

Contingency implies not only marginal relationships with family and friends, but also a longing for such relationships to resume from a better point than in the past or to take on their proper shape for the first time. From my observations, shame plays a key role in such longings. Through shame, the individual can sometimes spare himself the burden of final rejection. Shame can also be a face-saving tool for those already rejected by their families. With shame the door is open a crack. You wouldn't want to knock right now, but perhaps some day when you are doing better. If you can feel shame then you are still human and still eligible, in theory, for acceptance back into the family, for the help of people of your own blood, or the help of humanity as a whole.

One's family of origin can be a source of support, and extrusion may come after years of being sustained as the most vulnerable family member within straitened financial circumstances that threatened to take everyone under.[26] Families had tried to shield some of the individuals I talked to from becoming homeless, but those individuals nevertheless remembered the final break and a crushing rejection. Some talked about their own failings, pointing to incidents that both crystallized a long chain of events and made that chain appear less tangled, more sequential, and easier to break. Identification of the family conflict—lack of work, drug use, a dispute over inheritance—may be relatively accurate or distorted depending on the individual's insight, his current relationships with family members, and the version of events the family has decided upon or continues to fight over. In any case, perceived causation of trouble is not merely a rational taxonomy of events that happen near or far from us, but a form of what Snow and Anderson call "identity work."[27] Families were a source of support for some, of injury for others, and of both support and injury for yet others. They were the place to which many individuals looked back to make sense of their stories and create identities they could live with.

WORK AND MONEY

Many of my informants had significant work histories. One had been a custodian at Yale. Another had been a pipe fitter's apprentice at Electric Boat, a major defense contractor in Groton, Connecticut. One worked for a decade drawing blood at a medical laboratory, then started a carpet-cleaning business, then worked for another company. One had been a machinist. One had worked at the old Marlin Firearms factory in New Haven. One had been a day porter for a local bank.

There were many reasons for loss of work. One man was injured at his factory job. He was a heavy drug user at the time. A man in his forties who had done some construction work "had a nervous breakdown." He was attending an outpatient methadone maintenance program when I met him. A young man who worked at a gas station is a chronic alcoholic. The Yale custodian, a man in his mid-forties, used to get high and then stopped going to work. The pipe fitter was laid off in 1993, and that, he said, "really broke my spirit." He too has a drug problem. The man who had the carpet-cleaning business is also in his mid-forties. His business went under, and the next company he worked for moved south. And he too has a history of substance abuse.

My point here is not that these individuals are "in denial" or are making excuses (although they are, in part). Rather, it is that cause and effect can be a tangled web of associations and forces acting and reacting upon each other within and around the individual. Walter, the man who worked at Marlin Firearms, is a white male in his mid-fifties and a chronic alcoholic. He stopped working after his car broke down and his marriage fell apart. His car broke down because he couldn't afford a better one and his wife left him because of his drinking, which was a part of his family culture. Perhaps the trauma of separation and divorce made Walter drink more, although the actual split came after he was arrested for a drunken rage at home. Marlin Firearms was going under, and given his marginal level of functioning, Walter would probably have been among the first to be laid off if his car had lasted. And he might not have been able to keep any other job at that time because of his drinking. Walter may just have reached the end of his rope with his wife leaving him for another man, his car giving out on him, his sister screaming that his drinking was killing his mother, and his drinking getting worse.

Some individuals had disabilities that kept them out of the workforce. Of those, some had not secured support through federal entitlement programs such as SSI. For them as well as for those who were in and out of work, City Welfare was the inn of last resort. But in 1993 the city reduced General Assistance payments and stopped paying its clients' rent directly to landlords. The combination of a smaller payment and more cash in hand can be disastrous, especially for those with drug problems. Welfare programs are criticized for providing "disincentives" to work, but this is a partial truth that must be seen in light of the dismal alternatives available to most individuals on public assistance. "If I got off the city on a part-time job, the part-time job wasn't enough," said one man. "Once you got a job, you don't get food stamps, you don't get city assistance. Today, you have to have two or more jobs to survive."

Work is a practical matter. It can be the individual's primary source of income and a way out of homelessness. And work is symbolic of citizenship and respectability. Identity work, in relation to employment, involves plans and hopes for the future. Identity work, in relation to chronic unemployment, may involve explaining to oneself and others the futility of making any organized effort to change one's current situation. Ned, a forty-year-old African American, talked about what he saw as the homeless person's attitude toward his job prospects:

On a typical day sixty percent of you is saying, "I'm not going to worry about getting a job." Yet forty percent of you is saying, "I want a job. Where can I go get a job?" If you've been turned down a lot you're not going to worry about a job. You'll resort to hustling from day to day. Your mind is dumb and you lose hope easily after being turned down and not finding no work.

One man, standing at the imaginary gate of steady work, spared himself the futility that might follow such good luck:

You worry about eating. Sitting down, everybody's having lunch, you got nothing to eat till your first pay comes in. They hold back a week and a half. And then you gotta worry about your clothes, wearing the same clothes every day to work. Eventually you're going to start smelling, right? So that means somebody's going to say something on the job. The boss is going to come up to you and tell you to wash. What are you going to tell him? You got no place to wash if you're not in the shelter.

Peter, who spoke earlier about his Thanksgiving trip to Florida, was rare among the people I interviewed in looking beyond his own deficiencies or the limitations of local bureaucrats to more fundamental problems in the American political economy:

Welfare. People say its degrading. To me its more degrading for the government because you're showing people you ain't got the work. "Come to America and live the American dream." The American dream is: "Sit on your fat ass, man, and collect as little as possible because we ain't got the work." This is America? This can't be right in front of my eyes. Where's all the jobs? You're forcing welfare on them.

Peter may not quite believe his own rhetoric, though. He still sees himself as a marginal, contingent person:

I never crossed that invisible boundary that you would say "successful" and "unsuccessful." I describe it as at the finishing line but not getting over. You run the race and get to the line but you just don't cross, and that's been the story of my life.

Formal education held a magic for some homeless persons. Several identified their lack of education as a source of problems in the past and a barrier to making an exit from homelessness.

"If you don't have a decent education it's going to be harder to get a good job, and [you] wind up in a place like this," said one man. It is true that lack of education works against people, but its presence in some of those lives was associated with other mainstream pathways that had not been taken. Those who talked about the power of education and their failure to glean its rewards did not usually blame lack of opportunity, but only their bad choices at crucial points:

> I think it's out of my own stupidity of not doing something that I needed to do, like get my education on time. Immediately after going to high school I went to work doing this, doing that, and not doing things that would advance me into getting a better job, a better attitude about life.

Education is clearly a factor for success in a professional, service-oriented economy where unskilled work is scarce and pays less than a living wage, but education has symbolic value as well. It represents, for some homeless individuals, acceptance in society, but by itself, it is unlikely to grant that goal to the individual.[28]

DRUGS

Mental illness or addiction can contribute to marginality even when individuals are safely housed. When they are homeless as well, people are doubly marginalized. I was surprised at how few of my homeless informants talked about mental illness as a factor in their becoming or remaining homeless and how many talked about their past alcohol or drug abuse (though none about current habits). It may be that some see mental illness as irrelevant to their homelessness: the illness was in place while they were housed and is only exacerbated by homelessness. Then too, it is often one of the symptoms of mental illness that individuals who have it are unable to see it. One man who had been diagnosed with a severe mental illness told me how he had been singled out for fights in forty-seven of forty-eight states where he had worked, always ending up in jail because of the violent behavior of others. Other homeless persons, well aware of their mental illness, may not "admit" it openly because it has falsely defined their selves in others' eyes. This last possibility points to a distinction between the stigma of addiction and the stigma of mental illness. The addict can become an ex-junkie or recovering alcoholic at worst and a model citizen at best, but the mental patient is often seen as being stuck with his craziness. His illness carries with it a special shame and a more indelible otherness.

Drugs were a theme in many, though by no means all, of my informants' lives. Drugs affect everything in the addict's life, creating new problems and deepening those that may have contributed to the drug use itself. Drugs cause people to neglect their personal and financial responsibilities: jobs are lost, relationships fall apart, rent doesn't get paid, family and friends finally slam the door, and sometimes homelessness is the end result. All other goals—shelter, food, friendship, health, and the future—seem to fade for the hard-core user:

> I didn't care nothing about shit. I'd get out there and lie to my friends or so-called friends, even lied to my mom. It's crazy, cocaine is. It's the root of all things now. One time you used to hear about pimps, right? There ain't no pimps. You know the pimp out here? Cocaine. Cocaine pimps people's mother, their son, their father. You can destroy cocaine by water, you can try to bury it, throw it in a fire, but cocaine still around, it still pimping. The cocaine is still pimping.

Perhaps the overarching theme that came across in the accounts of homeless addicts was that of a complete break in trust with others, an obliteration of any remaining shred of a social contract between them and others while they were in the grip of their addictions. But some said that drugs and alcohol were also coping mechanisms, especially if they were sleeping on the streets.[29] Drinking can help you get to sleep at night or offer a momentary break from misery:

> You drink to keep warm when it's cold out. A lot of people say "Well you drank and you end up being colder anyway," but at

the time it gets you warm and it gets you out of the situation you're in. The same way for a crack addict. They can go into an abandoned building and get that fix. Even if it just lasts fifteen minutes, it's fifteen minutes that they don't have to deal with being homeless and figuring out "Where am I going to eat next?" or "Who am I going to steal from?" or "Where am I going to sleep tonight?"

That we can clearly see the rationalizations in such accounts need not keep us from acknowledging the truth in them. Nor does one have to be homeless to require a drink or a pill to get a little push off to sleep on a bad night. And bad nights can become a habit.

In telling their identity stories, some, like the next speaker, pointed to a fateful moment when the voice of temptation spoke and they failed to cover their ears:

My girlfriend died of an overdose and it affected me pretty badly. I let those people convince me that doing cocaine and running out all night was the best way to get away from feeling despair. I lost my apartment. Then I started IV use and that hooked me and then it was a game to obtain as much money as possible from different people by begging on the street or stealing things and selling them.

Identification of a point where "those people" led us astray implies the hope that a dismal situation can be turned around. If we can trace our way back through a thicket of oppressive circumstance, bad luck, and our own inadequacies, then perhaps we can awaken our old self and take back our lives. And people do sometimes take back their lives, if not from the place where they lost them.

NEGATIVITY

If one's home is "the outer envelope of personhood," then to be homeless, whether in a shelter or on the street, is to be "deprived of a measure of personhood."[30] Social setting, daily routine, family, job, car, friends, and the web of interaction that sustains and is spun from these elements create a safe environment for the self. We develop psychological buffers to protect us from being wounded by the day's petty annoyances. But the homeless person's buffers are stripped away from him on the streets. He may compensate by "getting crazy," since all of us fear deranged behavior. Deprived of physical privacy in an emergency shelter, he may create an invisible barrier of body language to keep others away.[31] He may slap on a fierce demeanor, or simply make no effort to disguise the rage and hostility that are already boiling up within him. Good behavior, after all, brings him no social rewards.

The stress, anxiety, and even loss of self that accompany homelessness may be caused in part by sleep deprivation and hunger, but a few nights in a warm bed and a few good meals in a pleasant environment are unlikely to vanquish the psychic damage of life at the edge, especially for longtime homeless persons.[32] The daily insults that must be borne and the feelings of impotence and fury that must be managed add up to an attack on the self. Any small disappointment or slight, imagined or real, can grow in the mind to assume the status of a major defeat.[33]

Some of my informants, like some researchers, argued that homelessness itself causes mental illness.[34] This "crazy-making" aspect of homelessness is a dual effect of concrete physical deficits such as hunger and lack of sleep, and the cumulative toll of anxiety, lack of normal social contact,[35] and loss of self-esteem. Ned explained how the lack of rest that plagues shelter people puts them at a disadvantage:

> Somebody that's coming from home, that's rested, they could relax and get away without being around other people. A homeless person don't get rest and you're up at six, out at seven-thirty in the morning every day. Rest is important. You're not rested up for what you go through mentally.

People said "you lose yourself completely" and become "a broken person." There is an "overwhelming feeling of hopelessness and the realization that you have no roof over your head," and a "feeling of pain, of being lost, of loneliness, especially loneliness." These feelings bring on depression and anger, at the world and with yourself, "like it's your fault":

> You give up a feeling of being a whole man. My spirit was broken, as a member of society and a man. I was a burden, a taker. This plays on itself, it fuels your lack of motivation and takes you further and further into dependence.

Many spoke of constant anxiety, worry, and irritability rather than of depression or sadness. Fundamental and practical questions pick at people:

> When am I gonna have this, when am I gonna get this? Are things gonna work out? Am I gonna be like this a long time? When is gonna be the day, when is gonna be the time? Does people want to be around me?

Negativity is the term that appeared most often in my conversations with homeless men and women. Negativity is both concrete and global. There is the negativity of "negative people talking about negative things" and the negativity of watching the "systems abusers" who have no future and make it harder for you to imagine one for yourself. There is the negativity of having "so much time to think and feed on the negativity of the situation and how bad you're doing." Negativity or irritability in the shelters comes from constant "nitpick" arguments, from the lack of privacy, from the rush and shove to get food or donated clothes, from the hard and monotonous routine of getting up early to walk the streets all day, or just from the fact and feel of being homeless with no exit in sight. Constant exposure to negativity and the inability to routinely find relief compounds its effects.[36] Some end up feeling that negativity has changed them permanently for the worse:

> It's hardened me. It's toughened me up—in a bad way, I think. It's made me tougher with society. Just callous. Making sure I got my end of whatever it was I was after. Clothes, food, goin' to a soup kitchen. Makin' sure I get my bowl of food.

And there is the negativity of scrounging for physical survival and not being able to piece together the essentials for maintaining your dignity. This is a pervasive negativity that infects your soul. Ned talks about this kind of negativity:

> There's negativity out here in the world. There's negativity if you got a job and you got a home. Just thinking about normal things that happen in the world or right here in this state where you live, it all boils up to more negativity than positive. For a homeless person that knows that and that gave up on themselves, there's not much hope 'cause that's what they see every day. I'm free, like Martin Luther King said. I'm free at last when I'm dead and buried. That's my freedom when I'm thirteen feet under, in the ground, with the plants on me. I'm free 'cause I don't have to wake up to face the negativity that's out here.

Michael Ignatieff's idea of an "equality of abjection that no man can endure"[37] captures an aspect of this pervasive negativity. Reflecting on King Lear's flight to the heath, the homeless otherworld of Elizabethan England, he writes:

> What respect, Shakespeare would have us ask, is owed a human being as a human being? It is one thing to answer this question in the zone of safety—in the castle, the family, the social world. There the humans we meet come clothed in difference, and the respect due to them is constituted by difference: by their wisdom, kindness, kingliness, natural authority, beauty, rank and stature. But what are we to answer in the zone of danger: in the no-man's-land of extremity, beyond family, beyond culture, beyond the safety of institutions which guaranteed the respect we owe to difference?[38]

Very little, it would seem. On the heath, shorn of the trappings of status and role that define us but also allow us to believe in the eminent domain of our inner selves, we find we are nothing but what we have, and what we have is nothing more than abject equality.

When I approached Peter about interviewing him for this study, I said I wanted to learn about the experience of homelessness. "It's not an experience," he said. "It's like if you have a woman, that's an experience. If you just think about having a woman, that's not an experience." For Peter, experience is associated with work and mainstream activities, with "being able to have a job, making money, have yourself a car." Experience is associated with earning what you get instead of taking handouts at the soup kitchen. "I prefer going to a restaurant or even some greasy spoon joint that you're paying for," he said. "Then you might know you deserve it. You earned that there heartburn." Temporarily unable to earn your living, you exist perhaps, but that is all. "I don't believe I'm having an experience. I believe I'm doing absolutely nothing. And there is no experience in doing absolutely nothing."

Homelessness, by Peter's account, is not a bad or difficult experience, and certainly not a world-transforming one. It is simply nothing at all. When I related this assessment to a colleague, he vehemently disagreed. He used Peter's analogy against him, citing a poem by Apollinaire on the anticipation of the sexual encounter to make the point that fantasy and imagination, the savoring of a possible future and the creative memory of a not-so-sweet past, are what give life its savor. A theory of experience that denies anticipation and the reconstruction of events is a negation of experience.

My colleague was correct by his lights, but Peter has his finger on another pulse. Reality, by Peter's lights, is what happens in the housed world because it has been designated as such by those who occupy that world. Homelessness is a loss of reality, a being bereft of experience—the shadow of being, compared to being itself. My colleague and the rest of us can make fine distinctions between thought and act because reality is defined inside the border, and experience inside the border is real in a dual sense: first, it is associated with an abundance of physical resources, and second, it carries with it the knowledge that physical resources stamp the owner as a possessor of reality. He who owns a piece of reality is human, and he who only thinks of owning a piece is not.

Homelessness, then, is a fringe state both internally and externally. Kidd, who spoke earlier, talked about radical separation and difference:

> I can pick out homeless people off the street. They have a different feel to them, a different walk, an aura about them. If you were talking about people in colors, everybody is red or what have you, and homeless are blue.

I had been trying to get Kidd to warm to the subject of the homeless experience. He had been parrying with me. I tempted him with his flair for metaphor:

Q. Are there comparisons you could make if you were trying to describe what it's like to be homeless?
A. Have you ever been really hungry for something? I mean obsessed hungry. Say you've eaten chocolate for a long time and you stop eating chocolate. Don't you once in a while just get that whiff of chocolate in your nose?

Q. So what do you have a hunger for when you're homeless?
A. To be what society considers quote unquote human. Because you're not looked at as a human being anymore.

Q. What do people consider being human?
A. (laughing) Being able to take a shower whenever and how long you want to or until the water gets cold. Being able to get up at eleven o'clock in the morning, or get up on a Saturday or a Sunday at three in the afternoon just because you want to.

Q. And that's what people consider being human?
A. Air, water, food, and shelter. You know, basic, basic needs . . .

Kidd, like Peter, associates mainstream life with physical comforts. Taken-for-granted amenities seem to have an almost mystical significance for both of them. Kidd is wrong about "basic needs" in the usual sense of the term. They can be met when you are homeless. There are emergency shelters to sleep in and soup kitchens to feed you. But the basic needs that are met by being part of the large inner circle of the comfortably housed are not merely food, shelter, and clothing. They are the security of belonging and of having your physical needs met at a reasonable level, and the knowledge that society has given its blessing to these effects. The homeless person may spend much of his time foraging for subsistence, but he does reflect on other needs, such as the need to be part of "what society considers quote unquote human." Snow and Anderson point out that homeless street people are part of a "superfluous population" without access to the traditional roles from which the rest of us draw our sense of self-worth and dignity. Identity needs, they argue, coexist with physical needs, even for those at the bottom of the material ladder.[39] The homeless person's reflections help him to maintain a psychological connection to reality, but they also reinforce his sense that he has been denied access to it. With reality come the trappings of identity; with the trappings of identity comes reality.

Ignatieff's "equality of abjection" and the negativity that accompanies it may also be derived from the institutional practices and values of key homeless stations[40]—shelters, soup kitchens, and welfare agencies—that homeless people contend with.

SHELTERS

The democratic ideal of the right to shelter with dignity is probably the best defense of "sheltering": everyone has a right to shelter from the elements regardless of why he or she became homeless. Given such a fundamental ideal, sheltering in its purest form is the antithesis of social service programs that go beyond meeting basic needs, common to all at all times, to address needs, such as job training, that are shared only by some at any given time. A second ideal of good sheltering, though, is to give people a helping hand out of homelessness through offering mental health and substance abuse treatment and other services.

It may be difficult, however, for the two ideals to coexist organizationally. Public mental health clinics that provide on-site treatment may be pressured by shelter administrators and staff to shave back on their goals and conform to the shelter's existing policies, which treat all guests alike.[41] The best shelters may strive to satisfy both ideals, but sheltering is a hard thing to do well by the standards we apply to social service programs that are not obligated to take all comers. The contradiction between the democracy of suffering for all and the alleviation of specific suffering may partially explain the sense of personal negation and injustice that many homeless persons share.

Many homeless persons resent shelter rules. One talked about "call-in" procedures at one of the shelters for guests who have a reserved bed but plan to come in late:

> I called in a half hour late to say I wasn't coming in. They A.D.'d [administratively discharged] me. No one explained the rules that you have to call in at a certain time. There was two people, one person was with me, and that person got away with it. I had to go out there in the cold for three days.

It can be difficult to sort out staff arbitrariness, guest manipulation of rules (the speaker just quoted says her companion "got away with" what she herself was punished for), and genuine confusion about policy. Each plays its part. In general, the homeless persons I talked to were more critical of shelter staff than of the shelter as an institution.[42] Many felt that staff abused their power or lacked respect for homeless persons' basic human dignity. The first speaker refers to a rule forbidding radios in the dormitories:

> All of a sudden she says, "Give me the radio." I said to myself, "What is this?" I'm a forty-eight-year-old woman and I don't feel that somebody in their late twenties should be speaking to me or anybody else like this. They're dealing with people who are left with nothing.

> Sometimes they treat grown men here like kids. Every individual that comes to those doors is first and foremost a grown indi-

vidual. No man is going to let you treat him like a boy. A lot of these guys that works here, you're older than they are.

It is one thing to identify staff with shelter rules and see them as enjoying the power they abuse. Here, at least, there is the veil of bureaucratic justice to stand between the supplicant and the naked face of staff power. It is another thing when staff rend the veil and engage in what homeless individuals can only see as a special, more personal negation of themselves. A homeless man talked to me about standing in line for dinner at one of the shelters:

> One night we're standing out there and there was a great lack of food. We were told, "One piece of chicken each, that's it." A staff member walks over, grabs three pieces of chicken. Look at them cross-eyed and they say, "Two weeks, you can't come back in." So nobody crosses them.[43]

Physical accommodations vary from shelter to shelter, but lack of privacy for sleeping, eating, or showering is a common complaint. Having to leave the shelter in the morning and come back at night is another. The physical hardship of being awakened at six after a bad night's sleep "around a lot of strangers" in order to leave the shelter by seven-thirty is exacerbated by the daily proof that one's personal story and needs are being swept away in a sea of negativity.

SOUP KITCHENS

New Haven is reputed to have some of the best soup kitchens on the East Coast. But eating has social and personal connotations that go beyond satisfying one's physical hunger. The following is from my field notes:

> I meet Patti and Jack, both outreach workers, at St. Ann's Soup Kitchen, reputed to serve the best free lunch in the area. You go down a set of steps to the church basement. The priest welcomes us all and leads us in a song: "Jesus in the morning, Jesus

in the evening, Jesus when the sun goes down." Most sing un-
enthusiastically or not at all. The priest gives thanks for the food
and prays, for us as well as for the people in Haiti, Somalia,
Rwanda, and Sarajevo who are not able to have lunch. Jack tells
me that when the priest's assistant prays he goes on for about ten
minutes.

St. Ann's has quite a spread today—meat loaf, corn bread,
green beans that are not overcooked, and chocolate pudding.
They have an unusual seating arrangement: the metal folding
chairs are turned upside down on the tables and you are supposed
to fill up one table at a time. Patti says people don't like it: "You're
brought up in a family. There's a meaning about who you eat
with. They make you sit so they can clear the tables in a certain
fashion to facilitate serving people. But people resist that. There
has to be someone who forces that to happen because people
want to eat with who they want to eat with."

Procedures vary from soup kitchen to soup kitchen, but all
such procedures have both instrumental and expressive functions.
Instrumentally, they help soup kitchen staff manage a large volume of patrons. Expressively, they reinforce, if unintentionally,
the message that eating has been reduced to its most elemental
physical function and stripped of its ritualistic social and spiritual
aspects. The following is from my field notes on another soup
kitchen:

The soup kitchen at Christ Episcopal Church does the biggest
volume in the area. Social service agencies send staff here to do
health screenings and offer other social services. Like any soup
kitchen, there is, by necessity, a common denominator feel to it.
Homeless persons talk about "being fed" and "feeding people."
Odd terms, but they seem apt today as I stand in line with about a
hundred others, the first wave of the lunch crowd. You come in
and you get fed. The person whose place you are waiting for is
being subtly encouraged to finish by the staff person who works
the tables. Your place, too, is taken the moment you get up. Looking at the line that has continued to grow as you eat, you understand that you have no business sitting here except to fill your
belly and catch a few more moments of warmth on a cold day.
A large, bright painting of a group of homeless persons hangs

at one end of the community room, but there is a drabness and thick depression in the air, as if people "were surrounded by a sheath of heavy air through which they could move and respond only at the cost of a deliberate effort."[44] I think of the similarity of this scene to accounts of the bread lines during the Great Depression. But now the bread line has moved inside. Perhaps it is because they are located indoors and out of public view that there is an air of permanence to soup kitchens today that (I imagine) was absent from the bread lines.

CITY WELFARE

Most homeless people in New Haven found their way to the City Welfare Department at some point in their homeless careers. (City Welfare in New Haven has now been taken over by the state, with new restrictions for receiving help.) Just as emergency shelter was the bottom rung of the housing ladder, City Welfare was the bottom rung of the financial support ladder for homeless people. Some homeless persons recognized structural constraints on compassion from welfare workers with large caseloads and no time to listen to the individual's story. Others were less generous. They talked about rigid adherence to rules when a little flexibility might have accomplished the putative goal of moving them off public assistance. One spoke of being made to feel he was taking money from his worker's pocket. Another heard the unspoken message that she could cheat as long as her worker did not discover her crime and have to do the paperwork that such an offense would invoke. Another commented on the different experiences of time of the parties to the welfare transaction: "When you try to get help, your needs are immediate— money, food. Your needs are now. They have a different time frame than you." For Kidd, the problem was untrained and unmotivated staff with bad attitudes:

> They're doing *at* their job, they're not *doing* the job. It's like saying, "I'll color the brick blue," then turn around and color it red, saying, "I did color the brick in, didn't I?"

While Kidd recognizes the lowest common denominator approach of many in low-grade social welfare positions, he omits two of its causes. One is caseloads that make high-quality work impossible even with the best training and education. The other is bureaucratic rules and regulations that make people-processing work relatively efficient but guarantee mediocrity. Workers understand the difference between *service* and *organizational* missions. The *service* mission of providing a safety net for poor people and helping them achieve self-sufficiency requires attention to individual needs and circumstances. The *organizational* mission of bureaucratic efficiency is achieved through treating individuals as members of categories. The service mission may call for the color blue or even different colors for different bricks, but this choosing and changing of paints and brushes is an inefficient way to run an organization that has too few staff and too few resources. Any color will do as long as the brick is painted, and the same color for all bricks will do even better.[45]

PERCEIVED INCOMPETENCE

Erving Goffman has written about the negative power of first appearances to help us fit the slightly odd into stigmatized categories.[46] Writers on the stigma of mental illness have argued that the label, once given, provides a damning reference point for the individual's future behavior, which is then seen to fit the label regardless of the fact that most of the individual's actions may conform to a normative model.[47] This process carries the seeds of a self-fulfilling prophecy, as stigmatized persons "organize their deviance" according to the stereotype,[48] participating in a "conspiracy of understanding"[49] about their identity that negates their chances of being or becoming anything other than what their stigmatized category proclaims then to be. Proponents of the "social breakdown syndrome" theory of stigma argue that individuals who cannot fulfill normative expectations, having been shown deficient in responding to environmental cues, paradoxically rely more and more on these cues, rather than on internal values, to guide their behavior. Anxious to get right what they have already got wrong, they find that their confidence in themselves and their values further atrophies as their social environment, which initially charged them with failure to perform, now signals that they are no longer expected to give a correct performance. Thus they are relieved of responsibility for their failure at the cost of proving the correctness of the applied stigma. A vicious downward cycle ends in setting them firmly and finally apart from others.[50]

A modified concept from complex organization theory may help to illustrate some aspects of these related processes as they apply to a compounding effect of homelessness—that of consistently negative contacts with mainstream society. Chester Barnard wrote that employees of large organizations use a "zone of indifference" to set aside their own judgment in order to follow their superiors' directives. Within this zone, employees will obey many orders that they would refuse in private life. When the order is so outrageous as to fall outside of their respective zones of indifference they will balk, but such instances are rare in organizational life.[51] Similarly, one could argue that the parties to most brief public interactions operate within a "zone of acceptance" or presumed competence, granting each other a fairly wide berth for demeanor, dress, and behavior and screening out much of what might strike them as odd or unacceptable. The more we sense that others grant us a zone of competence or acceptance, the more confident we are in our interactions with them and the more likely we are to fulfill their prophecy of competence.

That we assume a level of competence in the other is not a sign of our open-mindedness so much as a means for making brief public interactions possible. And this is a relative acceptance, to be sure: we adjust our behaviors based on signals of class, power, and proximity to our own interests. Still, something like a zone of competence appears to be in place for superficial interactions that make up a fair share of our public lives. Given initial signals of gesture or demeanor that all is not well, however, our taken-for-granted zone of acceptable behavior becomes conscious. The outsider comes under closer scrutiny and is found to be in violation. The violation detected, we actively interpret further signs and erect a barrier of presumed incompetence or disobedience against and around the offender. As violators, the more we sense the aura of a conferred zone of incompetence around us, the less confidence we will have and the more likely we may be to fulfill the other's prophecy of incompetence or willful disobedience.

For most of us, the perception of standing outside the norm comes at crisis points separated by long stretches of conformity to minimum social standards. But this crisis point *is* the norm for homeless individuals in their contacts with mainstream society and its institutions. For most of us, the counterweight to the responsibilities and stresses of mainstream life is an invisible chain of interaction and shared work that limits personal responsibility. For homeless persons there is relative isolation and no one else to blame. Their circumstance—being homeless—supplies proof of their incompetence.[52] Their flaws and failures are highlighted for all to see. Why, after all, would people stay in a shelter or on the streets unless they couldn't make it in society?

The perception of stigma and its fulfillment in action feed back on each other, giving repeated proof, for homeless persons and those who observe them, of the correctness of the stigma. Mainstream boundaries and structures put homeless persons in the way of what can be called "social traffic signals." Containment patterns and procedures that go unnoticed by most call for gestures of obedience at the margins by the few. For those inside the border, carriage and status constitute a prior appropriate response to most of these patterns and signals. Those at the margins may experience them as gestures of obedience of the soul.

An experience of my own as a displaced person at the New Haven Mall taught me something about this form of incompetence. I went to the Mall one afternoon to meet a homeless man who had agreed to tell me his story. He didn't show. Normally I have a purpose for being there: I meet people, buy them something to eat, set up my tape recorder, ask questions, and listen. Having a reason to be there, I do not think about needing one. But today I have none, so I decide to walk around. I realize how many security guards there are. I become self-conscious, and with this self-consciousness I begin to play the part of one who has a reason to be in the Mall. I review my physical makeup. Costume: am I well dressed? General appearance: am I unkempt? Demeanor: how purposeful do I appear? (This latter, more subtle performance is conveyed by expression, by a set of the jaw, by a stride that shows confidence and destination. My purpose must be seen as "shopping," but my performance may be challenged. If I have lost my purpose, what is my alibi, if anyone were to ask?) Associates: who are they, in fact or in the fantasies of my audience? The longer I am here and the longer I have to give this performance, the more tenuous my performance becomes. I pay more attention to my audience—primarily the security guards, but also the shopkeepers. I am also performing for the other shoppers (or those who are playing this role). Does my performance match theirs? As I become aware of needing to mirror and appease my audience, doubt and a low-grade fear creep in. My performance may be exposed as a sham. Conscious of my performance, I become false, and one whose performance should be ferreted out and judged as false.

Researchers of disaster and trauma have written about survivors' estrangement from the rest of humanity.[53] Those who stand inside the border may wittingly or unwittingly contribute to this sense of estrangement. Perhaps for many on both sides, homelessness is experienced not only as "a negation of the very idea of society"[54] but as a negation of life in its innermost essence. In the ancient rite of excommunication, the offender was banished from the human community. To experience a modern form of excommunication as the offender is a terrible thing. To contemplate the offender from within the border is a fearful thing as well, and a warning to the observer that he must not stray beyond the edge of the known world.

Homeless individuals talked to me about the public's fear of them and their own resentment at being lumped together as addicts and public nuisances. The following exchange occurred during my interview with a young homeless woman:

People look at us as subhuman, as almost not people. We're invisible. You ever watch anybody watch a homeless person and they don't see them?

Q. What do you think is going on in their minds? Do you think they don't see the person, or are they consciously deciding not to look at them?
A. Consciously deciding not to look at them.

Q. Why do you think they would do that?
A. Because I think they blame us for being homeless. People don't understand that it's society as a whole. It's demeaning to stand in line at the soup kitchen. You have people who volunteer, they genuinely want to help, but they look at you differently than they would one of their friends. I don't think they do it consciously . . . I don't like the term *homeless*.

Q. OK, talk about that.
A. Because it's more than not having a home. It should be *powerlessness*. Because you just lose every human right you can imagine when you're homeless.

What starts as public rejection may eventually be internalized, if it was not part of the individual's psychic constitution at the outset of his homeless career. But homeless persons are creative in coping with physical and psychological marginalization. Apt as Peter's "nonexperience" theory of homelessness may be, people respond to negativity by inventing experiences and identities to fill a void that human nature abhors. Even to advance the notion of nonexperience is partly to distance oneself from those who cannot name the condition and are therefore victims of it. One defense against negativity and perceived incompetence is pride. Among my informants, most of those who expressed a pride of survival were no longer homeless. One, a young white female who had slept on the steps of a church during a very cold winter, told me about the "secret" of homelessness. "They" in the following passage are the comfortably housed:

> They didn't live outside. They didn't experience the rawness and roughness of surviving alone. Just living outside, going to the bathroom outside, not having money. They don't know a secret: life isn't so complicated when you're homeless. You think about protection, being warm, and having enough food. You don't have to have a career. You don't have to have a job. Those things are not accessible at the moment, immediately. That's a little secret I got to experience. And I don't regret it.

A Vietnam veteran who was homeless for years before getting an apartment through the Veterans Administration still had no use for the middle class in their suburban homes:

> Those people are fools, working their asses off to keep other people rich, working at jobs that don't mean anything. I can contribute more being on the street than they can. I'd rather live on the streets than be like them people. They think they're free in their jobs and their houses. That's not a job, that's a sentence.

This man's statement sounds defensive, as though he is fending off society's judgment of him for having been homeless and now living in government-supported housing. But he is also reacting to society's ignorance of his accomplishment in surviving homelessness. His strength is a contribution he can make, but he has no forum for communicating this strength. A border of ignorance deepens the stigma of homelessness, even when the homeless person carries around his secret with pride.

Another defense against negativity and perceived incompetence is to distinguish oneself from one's compatriots.[55] A few of the self-described street people whom I met saw themselves as more trustworthy than shelter people. They took pride in possessing a measure of dignity and freedom:

> In the shelter nobody will help nobody. The people who live out of the shelter always help each other. They take care of each other with their money, beer, food, and places to stay. They take things in stride.

> We are the street people. Actually we're trolls. We live under a bridge. So we're the bridge people. There are guys in the shelter that will live there forever if you let them. And why not? They've got everything for nothing. But I won't do that. I won't live in a community thing like that where all they give you is a cot to sleep on. That's B.S. I'd rather live under a bridge and be free.

Some of my informants defined street people as those who panhandled and gave a bad name to homeless people. Some shelter users showed distaste for other shelter users. "Shelter people are institutionalized people," said one. They see the shelter as their home and "develop relationships with staff and get favors," learning how to get "two meals when the general population gets one." There was also, as a former homeless organizer parodied it, the mutual disrespect of addicts for drinkers—"Oh yeah, I get high, but I'm not walking around stupid all day slobbering"—and drinkers for addicts—"Oh yeah, I drink, but I don't have to steal or commit crimes." And there were racial divisions within the homeless ranks and between homeless persons and agency staff.

My point is not that these typecastings have empirical validity but that they represent, in part, strategies for distinguishing oneself within the ranks of the stigmatized. The homeless person who talks about homeless types is not only distinguishing himself from others and taking a higher perch in the pecking order; he is also reacting against the suffocating sameness of homelessness in his and others' eyes. Why should he not distance himself from the addict if he is not one? Why should he not distance himself from those who are numb and have given up all hope of leaving the shelter when he is fighting his own sense that this fate may befall him as well? It is hard to build one's identity if drink is no different from drugs and clean is no different from either, or if sleeping in a shelter is the same as sleeping on a windy ledge under Interstate 95.

3

Outreach Workers

Outreach work, broadly defined, is a practice even older than the wandering ministry of Jesus.[1] The story of modern outreach in America might begin in the 1820s, when Bible tract societies took on the challenge of defending the standards of a fading rural society against urban vice and godlessness.[2] Missions, storefronts, public halls, and warehouse lots became outposts for upper- and middle-class missionaries who promoted good morals through the example of their own lives and eradication of vice through holding up to the poor the mirror of their own degradation. In these evangelical forms of outreach there was a tendency to focus on individual flaws of the poor rather than on economic or structural problems in American society. At the outset there was ambivalence: Christian compassion for the sinner but censure for his sins; a zeal to transform slum dwellers and a complementary zeal to contain the spread of the slums.

By the mid–nineteenth century, voluntary organizations sent "friendly visitors" into the slums to distribute charity and help the poor to help themselves. Friendly visitors investigated the personal flaws of their charges, filing reports that served both as research data for more effective ministry and as tracking devices to keep individuals from obtaining charity in more than one place. In these visits to poor families we can discern the contradictory motives of sincerely felt friendship and manipulation that reappear in new dress in modern outreach. Paul Boyer describes the home-visiting technique:

> "Friendship" was of a special kind. Seemingly artless and spontaneous (when the visitor was skilled in her role), it was in fact

simply the necessary first step in a larger moral uplift process. For all the talk of neighborliness what was involved here was social control of an explicit variety to become a power in that home.[3]

The visitor's status as a member of a charitable organization was not discussed. Instead, one was a neighbor who wished to meet other neighbors. The work of the friendly visitor was built on deception, though a deception practiced for what the charitable organizations saw as the good of the deceived.

During the late 1800s, reformed alcoholics roamed the streets of urban slums and police courts looking for men who could benefit both from their message of salvation and from the jobs and housing at their disposal. By the turn of the century the Salvation Army, through its rehabilitation program, was enticing the poor with food, shelter, music, and uniforms. In these efforts we see a focus on flexibility and the use of multiple strategies and enticements—tools of the trade of contemporary homeless outreach workers.

The settlement house movement, in which middle-class females moved into the slums as more or less permanent visitors, was more liberal than its predecessors. Jane Addams criticized the manipulative techniques of friendly visitors from the charity organization movement, pointing out that the poor could manipulate in return by giving a show of moral uplift in exchange for food, rent money, and medical aid. Addams, backed up by the evidence of a devastating depression during the 1890s, eschewed a relentless view of the poor as the cause of their own problems. From both the Salvation Army and settlement house movements, we also see a relative shift from evangelistic to secular efforts, from voluntarism to an interest in broad government programs, and from a focus on the flaws of the individual to a recognition of environmental influences.

More direct precedents of modern-day outreach are "street" or "corner" work with ethnic youth in urban slums after World War I, later modified as "detached" work with youth gangs in the 1950s and beyond.[4] Detached work programs share themes with contemporary homeless outreach, including the idea that workers must bring their services to their clients since their clients will not come into the office.[5] The detached work strategy increased organizational flexibility, but also encouraged uncoordinated work with little professional supervision and no distinct philosophy beyond its eclecticism.[6]

Jim Baumohl notes that outreach of the sort done by ACCESS and other homeless outreach teams was practiced in American cities such as Boston, New York, Berkeley, and Seattle in the 1970s, sometimes as "acid rescue" in association with free health clinics and sometimes as outreach to vulnerable young women in association with runaway youth centers.[7] In the 1980s, urban mental health clinics, building in part on the Assertive Community Treatment (ACT) model of care for individuals who had been discharged from state psychiatric hospitals but were difficult to manage in the community,[8] began to provide outreach to mentally ill homeless persons. Many of these individuals avoid contact with traditional, office-based programs because of previous negative contacts with mental health agencies[9] or difficulty in gaining access to care.[10] Many deny their mental illnesses. Those who do venture into mental health clinics may, either because of the contingencies of homeless life or their own disorganized thinking, fail to come back for regular appointments, and be discharged as "noncompliant" patients. In addition, traditional clinic requirements for proper identification are at odds with the mores of street life, where contingency and anonymity are key values and where individuals trust only their closest friends with personal information.[11]

The workplace of outreach workers spans relatively tame shelters and soup kitchens and relatively unknown streets and highway bridges. Workers meet potential clients where they are—both geographically and existentially.[12] They have a healthy respect for their strengths as survivors of homelessness.[13] They do not insist, at the outset, that homeless persons accept mental health treatment, but help them to obtain food, emergency shelter, and clothing.[14] They slowly build trust with individuals in order to "engage" (make a therapeutic connection) with them and persuade them to accept mental health treatment.[15] Because mentally ill homeless persons have multiple needs, outreach workers must offer an array of other services such as substance abuse treatment, medical care, housing, and help in obtaining jobs or income supports. Homeless persons see outreach teams not only as treatment providers, but as a home base and conduit for ongoing treatment and rehabilitation services and for housing.[16]

Respect for individuals' strengths and for their wariness of mental health providers leads outreach teams to emphasize the ideals of client choice and working partnerships between staff and clients.[17] These ideals give object lessons in some of the ironies and dilemmas of outreach work.

The ideal of building on clients' strengths as well as correcting for their weaknesses represents a break with traditional mental health practice. The problem with this approach is that the talents which individuals employ to win a fast game of contingency on the street may not help them in mainstream society. A different pace and a different ability to read cues are required there. In addition, many social service programs to which individuals will eventually be referred are geared toward treating and managing their clients' *dis*-abilities. Thus, although drawing on individuals' survival skills is a worthy goal, it is difficult to put into practice.

The ideals of client choice and of the right to refuse treatment also represent breaks with traditional practice.[18] Homeless persons, especially those with a mental illness, who are alienated from mainstream institutions have somehow managed to survive on the streets. To help such individuals, the logic of client choice goes, you must offer them a partnership, not a caretaker relationship. You must give them choices from a full plate of services and respect their reluctance to accept mental health treatment.[19] In many cases, however, the client does have to give up the power to refuse treatment in order to make a gradual move out of homelessness.[20] And when negotiations break down in the dead of winter, the worker has the option of invoking the power of the state in the form of a psychiatrist who is willing to hospitalize the mentally ill client. Facing this dilemma, workers aim for the happy medium of educating homeless individuals about their need for treatment. Now, in theory, my wish to order what looks good on the menu and your wish that I eat a healthy meal are not diametrically opposed. I may welcome your suggestions and still make a "free" choice. But these two wishes are not the same, and our working relationship can founder on their difference.

STAFF SELECTION AND OUTLOOK

The outreach workers I interviewed were drawn to the work by their previous contact with homeless persons, by the opportunity to escape the structure of conventional practice, or by the attraction of the exotic and mysterious.[21] They were also drawn or pushed to the work by a chance for promotion or by agency needs. One senior clinician combined a taste for work in the community with the opportunity to move up one step in the state social service hierarchy. Other clinicians transferred to the outreach project in order to gain expertise in a particular subfield of mental health work. Others still came from the outside, securing coveted state positions when current employees chose to stay in their more prestigious office-based jobs. The nonprofit agencies that joined the outreach project employed individuals who had a similar range of motives: the chance, as newcomers, to gain experience in the social service field, or, as veterans, to move up or around within their organizations.

Community practice with the poorest of the poor has a less romantic and self-sacrificing side than its idealistic goals might lead one to expect. There are long coffee breaks, flexible schedules, and a relative lack of supervisory intrusion. Yet even with different career interests and social passions, the emerging values and demands of the outreach team virtually guarantee that those who are temperamentally unsuited for work outside the office will not stay the course.

Outreach workers experience a professional and personal identity crisis on the streets. Joan Shapiro, who studied social welfare work with residents of single room occupancy buildings in New York City, found that workers used "optimism, denial, and intellectualization" to overcome the anxiety of entering the alien world of the SROs. These techniques served as delaying tactics to overcome their fears and develop working relationships with SRO residents.[22] In New Haven, workers sometimes used moral support and rationalization to deal with the contradictions of middle-class life on one hand and street work with homeless people on the other. One worker talked about her initial difficulty in managing this contradiction:

> When I first started I had a hard time going home at night. I couldn't do anything that I usually did. I'd sit on the couch and think about what I was going through and try to think of ways I could get through it and not feel the guilt that I felt. When I came back from the weekend [clients asked], "How's your weekend, what did you do?" Did I glamorize what I did? Did I try to make it as dull as possible? Do you say, "I went out to dinner one night and bought some clothes?"

Finally, as this worker learned, you adjust to living in two worlds or you don't last long in the work. A compartmentalization of compassion helped workers to stay emotionally solvent as daily witnesses of homelessness:

> I talked to other workers, and they felt the same way. We helped each other. You have to come to terms with it. My home life is separate from what I do at work. You get used to it.

Guilt drives workers to seek support from coworkers and contributes to the development of esprit de corps. It allows them to distance themselves from clients and realign themselves with their middle-class roots. But guilt also allows workers to express their solidarity with homeless persons, since it emerges from first-hand experience that friends and associates do not share. And there are emotional rewards to compensate for the emotional demands of outreach. Having an impact on one person's life helps workers to carry on:

> The rewards can be overwhelming. I just had to fix my car, my ankle hurts, but when I see a guy lying on the street . . . I'm doing it for me. Because it makes me feel good. There's no greater feeling in the world than when you've had an effect on someone's life.

Workers' initial perceptions of homeless people are obviously important in shaping their future transactions with them. Daily presence on the streets educates workers to the effects of poverty and homelessness on their mentally ill clients' lives, and the interdisciplinary mixture of clinicians, case managers, and rehabilitation specialists helps workers to maintain a social slant on the work within a dominant framework of mental health treatment. Outreach workers know, for example, that even when their clients are able to work there are not going to be enough jobs for which they are qualified. One worker spoke about what she saw as the causes of homelessness: "economic factors and people who are on the edge." She continued:

> People with mental illness or some kind of disability are going to be the ones to fall first. It's hard economic times in Connecticut with businesses that have moved out, the way the city deteriorated, lack of low-income housing in neighborhoods that are safe. I think the guys living under the bridge are safer than some of the people we've housed.

Workers see the lack of access to cheap housing and the difficulty of maintaining a home as causes of becoming or remaining homeless. "Trying to stay in a house when people are living on City Welfare, the money just doesn't match the rent. It's a dollars-and-cents kind of thing," said one. "Lack of a system that makes it easy to get housing, have money for security deposits, and be able to pass credit checks," said another.

The workers I talked to also see strong links between their

clients' homelessness and their family histories. They meet individuals who are the black sheep of their families because of their mental illness or substance abuse. They learned of broken homes and physical and sexual abuse that resulted in people feeling "abused by the whole society." Homelessness, workers believe, compounds these problems, leaving people unable to manage all the things that come with having their own apartments, such as establishing and maintaining relationships with others. Some homeless individuals have "such traumatic home lives growing up that they associate being in their own home with that same experience, so that it's better to sleep under a bridge." Troubles in the family of origin, as one worker saw it, could have deep generational roots:

> There's people who have been brought up and have seen this pattern from generation to generation and really don't know that life doesn't have to be this way. They don't have the education behind them to make decent money. They don't have the family support. There are people that have grown up in homes without any rules. When you're an adult and you have to learn to live with society's rules, you don't know what the rules really are or how you follow them.

Some workers see substance abuse as a cause of homelessness, and lack of treatment as a barrier to escape. In the calm of the office, away from the abuse they sometimes have to take from addicts who do not meet the outreach project's admission criteria, workers can more readily empathize with these individuals:

> There aren't enough programs out there for substance abusers. They're angry. They feel lost and hopeless. The addiction takes over their whole personality. No matter what they really want for themselves, it's ten times harder because of their addiction.

Some workers agree with homeless persons and researchers who argue that drugs and alcohol can be tools that homeless persons use for deadening the pain of homelessness:

> There are people who have gotten lost in the system and don't know where to turn, so they turn to drugs, they turn to alcohol—

anything that numbs them up so they don't have to deal with what's going on inside them. It's easier to get through the day being numb than it is getting through the day feeling all that pain.

Others, though, rendered more conventional judgments about willful disobedience in substance abusers. The worker who earlier spoke on the generational influence in families of homeless persons had this to say:

> People that have substance abuse are in and out of homes because of their substance abuse. They are homeless, but they're more houseless than homeless. When they can pull it back together, they have somewhere to go.

Homelessness usually happens to people whose circumstances are radically different from those of outreach workers, but workers' empathy for all homeless persons can be deepened by meeting those whose prehomeless lives are uncomfortably like their own. One outreach worker talked about meeting a man who had worked for the telephone company for fifteen years, was laid off, and collected unemployment until his benefits ran out. This man went through his savings, got divorced, lost his house, and ended up sleeping on a park bench drinking alcohol. In building a personal identification with homeless persons, workers sometimes extrapolate from their own brief collisions with desperation. Bill, an African American in his early thirties, told a story that was closer to the bone than most:

> I worked at Bloomingdales and I had a financial mishap which left me homeless in New York for one night. I was going to get paid the next day, but I didn't have enough money to get my car out of the garage. I didn't want to bother my family. I said, "I don't have to work the next day, I'm getting paid, I'll hang in New York for the night." I went to the New York Public Library. It closed about nine P.M. I only had a few bucks, so I went to Popeye's Fried Chicken on Forty-second Street. New York prices, it didn't go far, just a drumstick and a leg. I went to Port Authority bus station. There were people with all types of skin disorders. One young lady had a stench because she had open

sores. It took three days to get it out of my nostrils, the stench was so strong.

The rule of thumb was you could not go to sleep. Once you dozed you were out. Cops would routinely check to see if you had a ticket. They had their nightstick and they would hassle people. I was well dressed and the cops looked at me. They were puzzled. I sat in one seat for hours because I didn't want to lose my seat. About two that morning they made everybody leave, all the homeless people.

Homeless people seem to migrate to some coffee shop. You're isolated, you're part of this migration. It was dark, the feeling. You didn't feel human. You felt like you were just acting the role as any other animal, just being part of the group. As far as your intellectual functions, there was no need for that. My priority was basic needs—to eat, get something to drink, to find safety. The coffee shop threw everybody out about three. I went to a magazine shop and looked at magazines for an hour. I ended up at Grand Central Station and watched the commuters come in, and by that time it was time to get paid. I was homeless for one night and it felt like forever, it felt like forever.

Workers are quick to point out the resourcefulness of homeless people. A psychiatrist spoke admiringly, even somewhat romantically, about his patients:

People we're seeing have the ability to survive on the streets. They're proud of that. They think this gives them a special view of life. They feel sensitive about their freedom and the ability to say no. The people we outreach have a specific need in not being forced to do something, not having any sense that they are subdued to a system. That makes a difference in the approach. It could be that they are less mentally ill than the people we usually see, or it could be that they have more strengths. I have a certain admiration for those people. They're accomplishing something which, I myself, I couldn't do it.

Another clinician echoed the words of the homeless woman whom I quoted, in the previous chapter, on the "secret" of homelessness:

I can imagine being homeless and getting through each day at a time and thinking, "I've survived another day. What a survivor I am." Looking at people driving by in cars going to their jobs, thinking, "They don't have it as hard as I do. I'm surviving better than they are. I have more odds against me and yet I'm still here day after day."

A few workers, the next one seemingly with a touch of envy, talked about the freedom of homeless persons from responsibilities that mark life in the mainstream:

> Homeless people, they're engaged in a lot of freedom. They live in an environment where their day is their day and it goes the way they like, as opposed to living in a home where you know you got responsibilities, you got bills, you got to work, just certain requirements you have that they don't have.

Most workers, though, see the experience of homelessness in shades of despair and disenfranchisement. "It's like you're at the bottom of the scale of life," said one. "Isolation and loneliness, separation from society, the sense of being an outcast or a nonparticipant in a world happening around you. An insignificant creature among this society whirling around. It didn't affect you, and you didn't affect it." Homelessness, workers feel, engenders a loss of self-respect, which in turn gives individuals an extra push downhill. The psychological and physical devastations of homelessness feed on each other.

IDENTIFICATION AND APPROACH

Outreach work is an odd mixture of entrepreneurial capitalism and bureaucratic people-processing. Workers go out to simultaneously sell their product to wary consumers and assess those consumers' eligibility to receive a limited but "free" product.

In mental health outreach work, prospective customers are identified by their stigmata. Outreach workers watch individuals in soup kitchens, in shelters, and in public places. Briefly observed visual signals and bits of information gleaned from others are used as a rationale for first contact. There are tip-offs that individuals are responding to inner voices or to visions: they talk to themselves in public, hold "conversations with the telephone pole or a tree," exhibit "strange posturing or gesturing," or laugh inappropriately. When one worker said that she looked for people who talked to themselves, I said I would qualify on that score. She elaborated:

> If somebody mumbles something to themself and stops, that's one thing. It's the duration of it, when they're talking in an extended way, and what they say, if they're agitated.

There are subtler shades of stigmata for the wise to read. Some people are "huddled up" or hold their heads down as if they are "shutting themselves off from the world." Others "sit off in the corner, isolated, their chair turned away," leading you to suspect that "they may be closed off." With these latter individuals, workers must collect further data by attempting to engage them in conversation "to try to probe and see what's really going on, the internal stimuli." Some isolated and withdrawn individuals are depressed. Others are quietly psychotic, looking around "like somebody is next to them when they're not."

While homeless persons who walk around in the summer wearing several layers of clothing may simply be carrying all their possessions on their backs, workers know that unkempt individuals wearing bizarre color schemes or an overcoat on a hot day are likely to be members of the "target population." People are also identified by their associates: "if they're with someone, if they're not, if they're never with someone, what you know about the people they're with." Sandy, a nurse clinician, looks for symptoms of physical neglect:

> I always look at people's feet and try to determine, Are they homeless? Do they have shoes? Do they look like they've changed their socks? Do they have swollen feet? Anything that's obviously been neglected, whether it's hygiene or physical ailments, clothing, shoes . . . A sense of neglect about something. People like John—he likes to be clean shaved, but he isn't frequently. You can see how he feels: has he taken the effort to shave?

It is a rule of thumb in the search for mentally ill homeless persons that those who ask for help early on probably do not qualify for it. "I look for the people who are off in the corners and isolated and quieter," said one worker, "as opposed to people more loudly approaching me for services and wanting something." The latter individuals are likely to be "hard-core" substance abusers.

Workers' most thankless task is that of rejecting people because they have the wrong disability. Delivering the bad news not only makes workers uncomfortable; it also carries with it the fear of danger from people who are fed up with rejection:

> I met somebody who was angry with the system and told me you had to be crazy to get help, that he's asked for help before and nobody has helped him. And people are telling him he's a lazy bum and he can go out and get a job.

Workers, in making their eligibility-by-disability assessments, also assess the physical and moral risk of approaching certain individuals:

> I observe the client from a distance first to learn as much as I can from observation. How they hold themselves. Are they threatening? Is this someone you should approach, shouldn't approach? How welcome might I be?

Difficult as it is to turn people away on categorical grounds, substance abusers' angry demands for services make it easier to deny them when the mute individual with schizophrenia is sitting off by himself asking nothing of anyone. Yet the categorical requirements given to workers are ambiguous. For one thing, substance abuse is regarded by some clinicians as a form of mental illness. For another, the interaction of co-occurring substance abuse and mental illness makes assessment of mental illness difficult even in the controlled atmosphere of the clinic. On the street, confounding factors of fatigue, survival behavior, and use of drugs or alcohol to cope with street life make accurate assessment even more difficult. Finally, distinctions between mental illness and substance abuse are not merely clinical but are bound up in our culture with moral distinctions that consider the degree of putative control the individual has over his illness and thus the degree of compassion he can expect to receive.

In New Haven, the categorical requirements outlined by the federal funding agency gave workers a ready justification for their choice of clients, but these requirements alone cannot assure their moral justification on the street. Workers must have other reasons for declining to help people who are simply homeless. One is that workers cannot solve all of society's ills and so are trying to help the most debilitated individuals. And there are others. But from my observations, workers are still morally uneasy about having to parcel out resources that so many need, even if they think their clients need them the most. One worker talked about the idea of eliminating mental illness from the criteria for getting help:

> You wouldn't have to observe their mental illness. They might not feel pinpointed or different from everybody else. It could just be whoever is homeless, there's services for them. That might be more acceptable to them, because being homeless is an economic issue, not a personal issue. They could focus more on "It's just the world of economics" rather than "It's me, it's all me."

These comments refer to the emotional difficulty of having to admit to mental illness for those who clearly have it. With a few changes in wording, though, they could apply as well to eliminating substance abuse from the criteria for getting help. That programs for all who are homeless would still be categorical, since the definition of homelessness would be the next contested terrain, and that such an approach would still separate homeless individuals from other poor people, are part and parcel of the contradictions and dilemmas of outreach work.

When bringing up the subject of mental illness, the workers I talked to are sensitive to their prospective client's feelings. They fear going too far too fast and losing a chance to build trust with the individual:

> People are frustrated that they can't control the voices or their own unorganized thinking. They are embarrassed that other people notice it, [that] it's not just happening in their head.

Workers often rely on euphemism and nonstigmatized terms with prospective clients to soften the blow of the fact that they need to be classified as mentally ill in order to get help. Here are a few examples:

> I try to do it delicately. Sometimes I won't even use the word *mental illness*. I'll soften it: "Sometimes have you felt that you needed somebody to talk to, outside of a friend, just somebody that didn't know you that would be objective?"

> I stress first that we're a project to help the homeless, and I soften the mental illness part. I try not to make it sound like you're crazy or schizophrenic but just, you have some mental health problems that you can use some assistance with.

> I use the word *counseling*. "Have you ever needed counseling?" Anybody could need counseling. And paying attention to how people react. I approach it gently. It's uncomfortable, but I'm finding that it's less uncomfortable as I do it.

> I frame it in general terms: "This is a project that can assist people that are homeless." If we've discussed counseling, I keep that separate. I let people ask the questions they are interested in. They'll say, "What kind of services?" "Well, what are the things you need?" "I want a pair of shoes," or "I need to see a doctor." People can usually say the thing that's foremost on their mind.

Jacqueline Wiseman has written that euphemisms may benefit workers more than prospective clients. The intention of workers to reduce stigma for their clients is tied up with their need to deflect hostility on the streets and with their use of deception in the name of providing treatment and housing. Deception can certainly be justified in some cases, but it places the worker in the morally ambiguous position of simultaneously espousing open, informal relationships with clients while remaining silent about key issues. Wiseman notes that prospective clients can employ euphemisms as well, misleading workers in order to disguise themselves as part of the target population.[23]

Having identified someone as eligible for help, the worker now has to approach the prospective client. Workers become contingency experts in pursuing the reluctant and wary. For this, flexibility and a good eye are key. Ed, a worker who had been homeless, talked about his technique:

> If they're unapproachable I might try to get them outside. If they smoke I might give them a cigarette. If they collect bottles I usually have bottles in my car. If I don't feel I could do it slowly—I'm not sure they'll be back—I'll go up and introduce myself and explain where I'm from and just ask them if they need any services.

Ed talked about his work with a man who was particularly difficult to approach:

> After getting to know this guy, I knew it was better for me to talk to him after he ate. It wouldn't do any good before. He was just a grouch, he would rebel and wouldn't want to hear anything. He was struggling with being able to feed himself. He didn't want to be involved with you if he hadn't eaten.

The initial approach—the building up of trust between the homeless person and the outreach worker—can take months or even years. Ed further described his approach to his reluctant client:

> I observed his survival tactics. I noticed that he picks up bottles. One of the things I did was collect some bottles. I brought the bottles down, using that as a conversation piece. He took the bottles. I observed that he had ripped-up blankets, so I offered him a blanket. He took the blanket. Every time we got together I had something to offer him. As time went on we became friends. I think the most vital piece that put a hook in him and drew him closer to me was that I would listen to him. I never asked him for anything, I always brought something *to* him. When he had been approached on the street they always wanted something *from* him.

Workers must be prepared to help individuals save face if they are too embarrassed to accept outreach gifts that remind them of their desperate straits. One worker talked about the contingency of face-saving:

> I may come across somebody in the park. I'd ask them if they want a cup of coffee. They say no in a way that you think, "They want it but don't want to be confronted with the fact that they're not able to get the cup of coffee on their own." At times like that I'm cautious.

The cup of coffee may not work now, but perhaps the worker can make another offer:

> Do I say, "We're from the homeless outreach team?" That just confronts them even more that they're homeless and we give handouts. I say, "We have an abundance of blankets and we want to get rid of them." Maybe they can hold on to it and give it to somebody that they know might need it. That way they can take it or not take it.

Any discussion of approach must take into account the physical characteristics of outreach sites. In New Haven, there are indoor sites such as soup kitchens, emergency shelters, welfare offices, the Mall, and the public library, and outdoor sites such as the Green, the railroad station, highway bridges, and other, less public places.

Most of the workers I interviewed preferred indoor sites for their initial encounters with homeless persons, primarily for reasons of safety and control. Workers develop relationships with staff at outreach sites, instructing them in the stigmata of mental illness. Having done so, they can often sidestep tentative approaches to patrons by asking these staff to identify and introduce them to prospective clients:

> In a soup kitchen or visiting a shelter I will ask, "Who do you think may fit our criteria?" and they'll point that person out. When there's a controlled environment people seem to be more willing to participate, even if it's just a conversation. They may

not want to talk to you but if someone has authority there and says, "Someone wants to talk to you and he's part of the ACCESS group," he says, "Sure."

Outreach workers sometimes worried, though, that these staff might dictate the tempo of their visits and limit their ability to approach people on their own. One worker spoke about staff at a particular soup kitchen:

> Usually the table that I chose to sit at would be determined by the staff. Clients have been targeted by soup kitchen staff, so we haven't been as free to explore other clients. Quiet psychotic clients, clients who are not having any observable symptoms— they get pushed to the side. We're always welcomed by the staff there, but they have an agenda for us: "That client over there and this client over there."

With the pressure to enroll one hundred clients a year as a requirement of the federal funding agency, checking in with soup kitchen staff became the most efficient use of outreach time at these locations. The success of the check-in approach also indicates the extent to which workers had been able to colonize homeless space by winning over those who managed the space. In doing so, the outreach project was in danger of losing its crisp edge of difference from other programs, just as improved assessment skills might deepen workers' clinical understanding while cushioning their encounter with the person and her story. For hard-pressed workers, though, an introduction from the soup kitchen director simply increases the odds of making contact. Workers also recognize that homeless persons are accustomed to seeing service providers in the soup kitchens and shelters. One more program and one more worker is nothing new. This familiarity gives workers a strategic advantage they lack on the streets:

> In a soup kitchen or shelter it's a comfortable situation. You have a chair to sit in. You're introduced: "The outreach team is here and they'll be up front to deal with your problems." At shelters

and soup kitchens they're used to having VA people or legal-help people or outreach people. They're available to help them with entitlements or whatever it is they need. There's an invitation set up ahead of time.

Soup kitchens have a lot of outside services come in: nurses, legal aid—things like that. They expect that. It would be different if you're going to a place where somebody was sleeping. It would be almost like going into their home.

There is moral comfort in the official sanction of being a service provider indoors. The safety of officialdom can also be reassuring to the potential client. "You're in a safe place, and they know who you are, that you're not going to harm them," said one worker. And the social atmosphere of eating, truncated as it might be in soup kitchens, offers workers more excuses for approaching people. Still, a complementary moral discomfort sometimes holds workers back. In the early stages of the project, workers had a tendency to observe patrons from the back lounge of one soup kitchen and set up office in another:

You set up a table and you sit there and have your paperwork in front of you and look like a provider of some type of services. You look like an official, somebody that's going to help them. That takes away skepticism. They're more apt to come up to you and find out what you have to offer.

All this is well and good if it works, but it fails to take into account one of the key tenets of assertive mental health outreach and a key rationale for funding outreach work in the first place— that the most withdrawn, alienated individuals will be those least likely to ask for services.

Workers have other reasons for making tentative approaches in soup kitchens. Much as food can be an excuse to sit down with people, the ritual of eating has deep personal and social connotations, and workers want to respect the privacy of this ritual, even in soup kitchens. To complicate matters further, one cannot assume that a given patron is homeless:

For me it's more socially uncomfortable in the soup kitchen because there's other people that eat in the soup kitchen than homeless people. So you need to have more information before you
identify clients. Approaching somebody who's actually sleeping
on the street, you already know they're homeless.

The difficulty of determining homelessness in the soup
kitchen can lead to some ironic outreach efforts, as one outreach
worker told me:

> This one client we were trying to target, watching, sitting next
> to her, having lunch and not knowing what to say to her . . .
> How was I going to get her some extra bread so she could feed
> the birds on her way home from the soup kitchen? I'd start con-
> versations with her about feeding the birds, and the relationship
> progressed over time. [Then] we found out she was not home-
> less. She shared an apartment with her sister.

Mental illness is a stigmatizing condition in the homeless as
well as the housed culture, and workers worry about approaching individuals in front of other patrons in the soup kitchens.
Identification as a mental patient can further isolate individuals
or subject them to manipulation by their peers:

> Because our target population is the mentally ill homeless, we
> don't want to stigmatize anybody or let the general population
> know we've identified them. Maybe that's why we let them
> make that decision to come to us.

There are ways to get around this dilemma, as the last speaker
found. This involves taking a more general approach:

> I walk around the whole soup kitchen and say, "Good morn-
> ing." So by striking up a conversation with the general popula-
> tion, if I single out a mentally ill homeless person it doesn't look
> so obvious because I'm talking to everybody.

Even so, it appeared that social service ownership of space was
mostly confined to the back rooms, side areas, or offices of soup
kitchens and shelters. The office continues to exert its lure, even

for the most adventurous workers out on the frontier of professional practice.

The physical layout of indoor sites partly shapes the interactions of homeless persons and outreach workers. Workers are
relatively comfortable or uneasy depending on how much room
they have for maneuvering, how much they are on view when
they walk in, how much the space lends itself to observation, and
other factors distinct from the nature of the clientele that oc-
cupies the space. Soup kitchens, for example, seemed to be more
uncomfortable sites for workers than a local homeless drop-in
center, although the mainly drug-using clientele at the latter was
among the most demanding and difficult to work with. At the
time of my research, the drop-in center was housed in a large,
open storefront with no offices and few physical resources. There
were strategic waiting points at the peripheries from which one
could approach patrons, grouped in easy chairs around the tele-
vision set, at an opportune moment. The exits and entrances
were under less moral scrutiny, by fewer observers, patrons, and
drop-in staff, than at the more cloistered soup kitchens. Ironi-
cally, the fact that there was less density to the patrons' space and
thus less discomfort for workers made colonization more difficult, since it was harder for workers to mix with the crowd and
quietly send the waves of their influence into a sea of potential
clients.

The physical space at soup kitchens is dominated by tables
and lines of people waiting to be served. Workers shed some of
their professional insulation when they go out into the field in
casual clothes. They may use props such as a flyer with information about their program when they approach people, or they
may, as I noted earlier, ask soup kitchen staff for an introduction
to a patron. The space itself cannot not help them, and "going
native" by standing in the soup line and eating with the regulars
is simultaneously a lonely and an intimate experience:

> The soup kitchens are comfortable safety-wise and not socially,
> and on the streets it's the other way around. In the soup kitchen
> there's other people. And usually, even though you can dress

down for the occasion, they have some sense that you don't belong there. It's uncomfortable to sit at a table with a client.

Workers also observe the emotional rawness of coed soup kitchens, where sexual tension is colored by the fact that many women who eat there have been victims of sexual abuse at the hands of men. The exterior gathering spots for indoor sites sometimes have a moral and cultural feel quite different from their interiors. Outside one soup kitchen, people gather before and after meals in an alleyway between the soup kitchen and a drive-in bank teller. For workers, several things change their relationship to the space and its occupants: their purpose, such as checking out the site or actually approaching individuals; their status, such as known or not known as a worker; and their physical position, such as standing or sitting at the edge or in the thick of things. Sitting near a patron at the curb may be the most effective outreach approach to take at a given time. The following is from my field notes:

> Patrons gather in small groups or sit off by themselves until the meal line forms. Sometimes they hang around after eating. Sitting on the alleyway curb, I talk with Jamie, a thin African American man of about forty. With his missing front teeth, his unhealthy-looking skin, and his disheveled clothing, he has a forbidding, even dangerous appearance. He is harmless, though. He says his troubles stem from his wife's involvement with voodoo. She was "deep in the doctoring of the skadootz." This could be voodoo terminology, and Jamie's slurred speech could be caused by his lack of front teeth rather than drug or alcohol use. And he can be lucid about his needs and desires. He doesn't just want things done for him: "I want to do something for me before my eyes are closed." This includes getting a job, and Jamie has worked between bouts with mental illness and drug addiction.
>
> I sit down next to Elijah Bologna [his real name is similarly flamboyant], a maybe homeless but apparently hard-core substance abuser who wants to get an apartment through the outreach project. I feel as though I'm taking part in a ritual performance as well as a negotiation for services. It's as though each of us knows his proper role and that if our performance comes off

smoothly, it will be a satisfying social exchange, if not a satisfying commercial one. The performance is built around whether Elijah meets the outreach project's criterion of having a bona fide mental illness ("I have hallucinations. I really want to talk to your psychiatrist"), and whether he is willing to get treatment for his substance abuse.

We assume that Elijah's last name is his little joke to tell us what he's full of. [Two years later his brother became a client of the outreach project and we learned that Elijah's last name really was what he said it was. Such revelations are salutary for the jaded outreach worker.] Elijah makes small talk with an attractive woman and plays with her young child. As they are leaving, he pays back the woman some food stamps he owed her.

The alleyway is a marketplace for homeless and other poor persons, a site for brief social and commercial interactions and for exchanging information on the day's events. Outreach workers can sometimes work their way into this marketplace to display their own more substantial mainstream wares.

Street outreach is different. "To engage a person on the street is more difficult," said one worker. "There are less controls. The individual is able to isolate you." For many workers, the streets are not only physically but also morally and culturally less safe than indoor sites. There is an intrusive quality to initial meetings. The workers I talked to often felt that individuals they found outside wanted to be left alone. It was harder for them to justify violating such wishes on the street than on what they saw as social service turf. A worker commented on the unknown nature of street encounters:

> If I meet someone under a bridge or in a parking garage or on the street, I'm a stranger to them until I identify who I am and they trust that I am who I say I am.

Street outreach is a broad term that belies the variation in public space it encompasses and the range of moral and physical safety it affords. For example, the most public outdoor site in New Haven is the Green. The New Haven Green is crisscrossed by gravel paths and lined on its perimeter with maple trees. Stone benches with wooden slats are anchored along the paths, and Paris *métro*-style shelters with black steel frames and smoky-glass roofs stand near the stops for the buses that kneel for handicapped people. The Green is ringed with the Episcopal, United Church of Christ, and Methodist churches that have stood here for as many as two hundred years and by the New Haven Public Library, the New Haven Superior Court, and City Hall. A few years ago the Green housed a tent city. Now homeless people sit on benches during the day and sometimes sleep here at night. The police are tolerant, but the Parks Department will confiscate unattended possessions once the Christmas tree is raised in December and the lights go up. Workers approach people who are sitting on benches or walking by on the paths. If rebuffed, they can apologize and move on. They see the Green as private space, the homeless person's home:

> It's on their own territory. You're in their house—that park bench, that box, that alley. You need to invite yourself in a different way than you would in a soup kitchen or a shelter. You're on a more equal par when you're out on the street with someone. I think a street encounter is the unexpected. Street outreach is more intimate. It's the client and you, not other people.

Street outreach can be far more private and potentially dangerous than that done on the Green. Work in out-of-the-way sites is simultaneously the most attractive and repellent part of outreach work, and the stuff of which the romance of outreach is made. Consider the abandoned parking garages where some people sleep. Near the thick concrete columns that support the upper levels of the abandoned Macy's parking garage, there are binlike enclosures where people store clothes and liquor bottles. Workers' calling cards are mixed in with plastic wrappers and old newspapers. Down one floor on the basement level there are the same binlike enclosures, some empty, some filled with clothes and papers and maybe an empty liquor bottle. The basement-level bins are more isolated and give protection from the rain and wind in bad weather. There is only one visible way out—

the narrow stairway you take to come down here—although there may be another somewhere in the dark beyond where workers stand.

Or consider the highway bridges. The Interstate 95 bridge over Water Street stands in a run-down industrial section of town. You think of rain even when there is none. There are ledges on the underside of the overpass. Blankets are neatly folded. Sometimes there is a photo or two pasted on the steel undergirding running over the ledge. There is an almost military neatness and precision to the bunklike arrangements. Indeed, a good number of the men who normally sleep here are veterans. Workers leave sandwiches and business cards. They approach men (and they are almost always men) carefully until they know them well, making strategic decisions about whether to wake them based on the feel of the situation and any information they have gathered about the sleepers. Often, the men have left by the time workers get here.

And there are other out-of-the-way sites. Workers scramble down a steep grassy hill to a path leading to a viaduct that forms part of a busy street near downtown New Haven. They hesitate, not seeing what lies ahead, but the closer they get the more they can see the entire width of the passage with light at the other end. At one time a line of mattresses marked the middle of the viaduct. People would leave jackets, mattresses, and sports bags here, although they have to be prepared to move on or hide their belongings when out-of-the-way sites become popular.

At times, physical and cultural danger and fantasy collide to produce encounters with deep resonance for workers. The following entry from my field notes describes an early encounter for the New Haven ACCESS outreach team:

> Jack, Allen [both outreach workers], and I walk down the entry ramp to the abandoned underground level of the New Haven Coliseum parking garage. There is a sickly yellow light from overhead lamps and an indescribable smell with staleness and mold in it. At our left is a loading dock–like opening at shoulder height with about an inch of water on its floor. We look in-

side. It appears to run downhill and parallel to the ramp. There are no rats in sight but we are ready to kick one. The ramp we are walking down curves to the right and then takes a sharp left. We lose sight of the street above. Past the curve a concrete retaining wall about twenty feet in front of us obscures our view of what lies behind it. This is as far as any of the outreach teams have gone. At our left there is a metal door that, we surmise, is the far end of the loading dock that we passed above. Allen opens the door. A man with black-rimmed glasses is lying on a bare mattress with a blanket up to his chin. He looks out at us. Allen asks him if he'd like a cup of coffee or a sandwich. A sandwich, he says. Allen gives him a sandwich and a calling card and closes the metal door. We walk back up the ramp to the car.

Allen did not knock before opening the door. On the way up he gave voice to what we were all thinking—that this man could have had a gun and blown us all away. Was he mentally ill? On the run from the law? We never saw him again. This encounter, along with others, prompted discussions about staff safety that led to protocols for investigating new outreach sites and limitations on outreach in less protected sites. It also prompted more symbolic reflections. Opening doors became a group metaphor for safety and danger, for the unknown world of the homeless person. Also for what constitutes a home, what it means to cross the threshold, and how far workers can or should or are willing to go in their rescue efforts on the streets.

ETHOS

In early outreach work, I observed the emergence of an occupational ethos in which values and technique were intertwined. Workers have visions of their roles that go beyond the work itself. For some, it is educating others by explaining "that people aren't homeless because they want to be." For others, it is "having someone see what you're doing, maybe build up their curiosity to think of why you're doing this." One worker seemed to feel that his work partly compensated for the public's isolationism:

We've gotten to a point where we're so concerned about ourselves and our own orbit. I go home, my dad doesn't know his
next-door neighbor. When I was growing up we stayed over.
People don't reach out to each other. They're leery of others.
And they're probably leery of you. It feeds on itself.

Human compassion (sometimes colored by the individual
worker's spiritual or religious beliefs) and social liberalism often
went together. Bill, who earlier told his story of a night spent
homeless in New York City, talked about the need to move away
from a deserving-undeserving dichotomy for doling out compassion and services:

> There has to be something to revitalize the souls of people and
> their aspirations and dreams, to give them a sense of worthiness
> in society. I think the voice of the homeless person is not just
> their voice. Veterans are saying the same thing: "Listen to us."
> The elderly . . . Look at the money that's being wasted to pro-
> cess a criminal through the court system, jails, to imprison some-
> one. We can use those monies for more effective approaches to
> our life. We just can't keep having twin societies, the good and
> the bad. We're all interlocked.

Bill believes that ultimate responsibility for the problem of
homelessness rests in Washington, which has the moral authority and power to set the national agenda. He also believes that
individuals like himself can help to break down the split between
putatively deserving and undeserving homeless persons:

> The national agenda doesn't have to be Republican or Democrat
> but citizens. I think everyone should have some cause to advance
> our society. If we can provide services to an individual who's un-
> able to care for themselves, to be a productive person, not just in
> producing some great advancement, but to themselves, it's like
> throwing a stone into a pond. It has an effect on all of us.

This liberal vision of citizenship helps to shorten the cultural
distance between worker and client and unite them in a mythical republic of personhood. Bill explained:

> Homeless people have a past. A person's history, their actions—
> it's all information. Like, "He picked up a fork." It might have

been an individual who hasn't used a fork in ten years. They're giving us an opportunity to look into their world. It's like a reflection, a mirror. It reflects what we are and what we hope not to be.

Visions such as Bill's allow workers to acknowledge and yet undercut otherness, to define their leadership in relation to lost individuals and give a transcendent justification to the work. Workers are acutely aware of the need to offer tangible resources, whether cigarettes and coffee or an apartment, to homeless persons. But compassion is a sine qua non of the work and is seen as a collective commandment as well as an individual value. Such a commandment, valid as it is for this work, might be expected of a mental health outreach project that must define its task in relation to its clients' affective and cognitive deficits. It also helps to cover a multitude of qualified successes and some failures, but it is always in danger of being exposed as false if workers are unable to deliver tangible as well as emotional resources to their clients.

For workers, there is a "specialness" about outreach work and the people who perform it and a corresponding sense that many others cannot be counted on to genuinely care for homeless individuals. People-processing work, such as that performed by City Welfare caseworkers, breeds contempt for the client and identification with bureaucracy, workers feel. Ed, the formerly homeless worker who was quoted earlier, spoke from experience about being an object of contempt:

> When I was homeless, in the office they treated me like a client; everything was all right. When I saw them downtown, they acted like they didn't know me. A lot of clients face rejection when they're outside of the office. You have to be one way with them. Either you care about them or you don't.

Some workers acknowledged that welfare caseworkers operate under severe constraints:

> They don't have time to see why you're on the street. "You missed your appointment." "You didn't bring that document."

"You didn't . . ." I think some are really concerned but don't have the time or don't want to take time to be sensitive to each individual: "This is a job, I have to do it."

But this attitude, born under bureaucratic pressure as it might be, is not tolerated by outreach workers. "Someone who does not have compassion or understanding does not belong on this team," said one. Another said simply, "We are different." An analysis of outreach work must look not only to its roots and techniques but also to its emblematic character. To call oneself an outreach worker is to make a political and professional statement that one is allied with the poor against soulless bureaucrats. The tendency to compare outreach work with programs, such as City Welfare, that fail to put the principle of caring for unique individuals into action is a powerful organizing factor for outreach workers. Two expressive and instrumental rules of outreach—having compassion and knowing your resources— simultaneously give staff the heart to go on and fire their image of themselves as the people with heart:

> Some nights we were off the clock, and on our way home we would go under the bridge. We would bring blankets, extra stuff that we had. Off the clock. One thing I learned from dealing with my clients and working in a position of this nature is that you have to have a heart, and you've got to know your resources.

> The two main qualities are compassion and knowledge of the resources. If you're just coming to collect a paycheck you may overlook [a severely mentally ill] client and go to someone that's easier to talk to. You're rejected many times. Compassion helps you overcome your feeling of rejection. The reward you get is the one good one. You're going to lose some people . . .

Having compassion and knowing your resources gives workers little comfort without a number of successes to go with some failures. Workers' satisfaction comes from the instrumental aspects of the work: finding an apartment and money for a veteran who has lived under a bridge for years, persuading an individual with a severe mental illness to take medication, or taking a woman with a bad limp to get medical treatment she has avoided for years. It also comes from seeing a spark of life in one who has worn the blank mask of desolation from too many years on the street. Bill talked about the change in one client after workers persuaded her to move into an apartment and accept mental health treatment:

> I've seen Andrea come to Columbus House, and she seemed to be so oriented. It was a day when she was really on. Things were in place, and if I didn't know her history I would have viewed her as being a sane person, someone who had no issues of mental illness. A lot of Columbus House staff made comments on how she had this incredible glow. You could feel some life force had come back into this woman's life.

Outreach workers cherish another key principle in their early engagement with homeless persons and their later work with them as clients. This is, simply, "Don't make promises you can't keep." Promises made in the early stage include both the consistency of being in a certain place at a certain time (even if the prospective client is not) and of delivering the promised goods:

> If a client says he needs a blanket and you say, "OK, I'll get you one," and then you don't get it for a week, this client could freeze out there. I think a lot of these clients look at, "Can this person really come through? Does he have the contacts or the resources that he says?" Once they see you come through they build a confidence in you and they start dealing with you more.

Later, keeping your word involves giving yourself plenty of leeway on the delivery date for promised goods. This can be a lesson of bitter experience. In New Haven, workers fired off applications to a new rental-assistance program for homeless persons, only to find that bureaucracy could move at the same pace for people sleeping under bridges in the dead of winter as it could for others at any time of the year. One worker, having been burned by her enthusiasm and naïveté, vowed that she would not repeat her mistake:

> I'm careful not to make promises I can't keep, not to give time frames, especially in housing. We don't know if they'll be able

to get housing. I can't say, "Within the next week or the next month," because of all the bureaucracy.

The fundamental principles of following through on promises made and not making those you can't keep may be the best guides that staff can give themselves. They are in keeping with the spirit of the work and homeless people's skepticism. But the demands of the work place workers in constant danger of violating these principles, as caseloads rise and the needs of homeless individuals are ranked against those of other client groups.

One worker observed that you have "crossed a bridge" when the individual begins to tell you his story. The story, which is the person, became a powerful symbol for the outreach team. It is a clinical concept in that it is necessary to come to terms with the client's history in order to treat him. It is a humanistic concept in that it conveys belief in a recognizable, if harrowing, past behind "others" who seem cut off from all human contact. And it is a spiritual concept in that it imbues homeless persons with the mystery of human suffering and workers with a sacred responsibility as healers.

I asked one worker how he was able to gain entry to the homeless person's world. He gave this reply, in reference to a homeless woman he found sleeping in an abandoned parking garage in downtown New Haven:

> Unconditional positive regard. Andrea was eating out of a garbage can. Giving her a hug was what got her to trust me. Cindy [another worker] was repulsed by her. Andrea said, "The reason I trust you is that you never treated me like trash."

Other workers used similarly idealistic terms to describe their outreach techniques. Bill compared his outreach approach to that of a sacrifice to appease the deity:

> I find most people are approachable out there. What helps is when you have something to offer, a peace offering of some sort. Doughnuts, or coffee or a sandwich, really carries a lot of weight. I'm aware of different types of offerings and the sacrificial sys-

tems that were used by the Hebrews, where God wanted to be appeased by some form of sacrifice. You have to give up something in order to gain something. There has to be some value to it. It's not how big it is but what does it mean to the individual.

Jacqueline Wiseman wrote about the Christian symbolism of sin, redemption, and eventual return to society in the staff-client encounters of an earlier era of homelessness.[24] One can detect at least a trace of these elements in mental health outreach, even when workers, like the one quoted earlier, espouse no specific religious ideology. This is not to say that workers regard their clients as sinners or themselves as missionaries, but that such themes are rooted in our culture and to some degree in the ideologies of professional helpers.

More experienced workers eventually confront the contradictions of humanism and clinical persuasion. Compare with Bill's words those of a veteran worker from an outreach project in another city:

> I'm a salesman. I have a product to sell. And to sell I must have a gimmick. I'm not bringing food, I'm creating dependency. Goodies help people give up the freedom of street life and mental illness without medication and side effects. We think the emphasis is on the humane thing and it's not. The humane thing is only a tool to make you successful in helping this person who is in that bad situation. This may sound opportunistic, that you're manipulating. Guess what? You are.

The worker who made these comments also spoke eloquently about the "humane" approach, but insisted that workers confront the impurities of outreach work. Her statement echoes Wiseman's assessment (and Boyer's, on friendly visitors of an earlier era): the atmosphere of friendship is contrived, a tool for engagement with the client. Workers are paid to be compassionate.[25] Going off the clock means being on the clock most of the time, engaged in the business of empathy. There is nothing new in this, of course, and being paid to help does not mean that workers do not genuinely care for their clients. But work with the poor outside the four walls of the institution seems to demand higher allegiance to the client and to push workers toward a purity of heart that is difficult to achieve or maintain in practice. This worker's statement implies the paradox that outreach work is simultaneously the most natural and the most contrived form of professional help. The contradiction of the natural and the controlled can be seen in the oddly military terms—outreach and engagement, enrollment in services, and transition or transfer to continuing treatment—that name the stages of the gentle process of outreach work. Workers must live with the contradictions of their friendly yet manipulative approach. They do so by faith in the clinical tenet that mentally ill homeless individuals are sometimes unable to make judgments that are in their own best interests. Rooted deep in this tenet are the images of a loss of humanity at the border of society, redemption through the loving intervention of rescuers, and finally, a return to society as a human being made whole again.

4

Boundary Transactions

The boundary encounters described in this report are events in which services and identity are negotiated. Homeless persons weigh the offer of housing against the uncertainties that go along with becoming housed persons. They bargain with workers for tangible goods; workers sell treatment and medication to go with these goods. Workers seek to expand their territory, homeless persons to protect theirs. Homeless persons seek a sense of belonging; workers seek to be the experts, friends, and even the heroes who provide it. Workers pursue homeless persons in order to fulfill the requirements of their jobs; homeless individuals who lack the proper disabilities may paste stigmata on themselves in order to qualify.

Homeless individuals bring to these encounters a pattern of coping built on the skillful use of contingency, a negative experience of homelessness, and a sense of being rejected by society. Workers bring a crusader's passion and the belief that empathy and tangible goods together will enable their clients to escape homelessness. The full package that workers offer is available only to individuals who accept treatment and the idea that treatment will become integrated within the fabric of their lives. But homeless people, as Steven Segal and Jim Baumohl observe, may use treatment and ancillary services as therapeutic rest stops rather than as ends in themselves. Inpatient hospitalization may mean refuge and recuperation rather than treatment. The clinician may be an adviser who can also be trusted to receive and hold one's mail rather than a "treater." This does not mean that homeless people misunderstand the official purpose of these resources, but that they may redefine that purpose in order to meet their needs and to eschew institutional definitions of therapy or the label of mental patient.[1] When the perspectives of helper and helped are radically opposed, however, there is a danger that one party will reject the other's advance.[2]

MUTUAL PERSPECTIVES

HOMELESS INDIVIDUALS

Homeless individuals are often wary of outreach workers who offer a cornucopia of jobs, income support, housing, medical care, and mental health and substance abuse treatment. The fact that workers are actively pursuing them to boot may strike some as too good to be true. "This must be a joke to get some kind of information to put us down," said one man. (Indeed, the New Haven ACCESS project was collecting a great deal of research data on its clients.) Another man sat through the research intake and baseline interviews for the national study and agreed to have his photo taken to facilitate sightings of him for follow-up interviews. When talking with me, he compared this process to a police sting, even though the interviewer had explained its purpose to him:

> How come they took my picture? They said, "In case we're lookin' for you." Things run through your mind. Maybe it's one of these gimmicks they got, they get people with warrants on them: "You won this here, we're having a big party," and all these people with warrants go there and boom, they make a sweep.

The next speaker eyed me suspiciously and got up abruptly to pace around the room during my interview with him for this study. A clinician would probably point out elements of paranoia in his behavior, but his analysis of the negotiating process between workers and homeless persons showed a shrewd insight into the politics of homeless services:

> I know what ACCESS needs. They need me to keep the project going. Otherwise the project would not have succeeded to

where it got now. I'm the one they need to feed them the information about the city, the people, what's going on. They need somebody they can experiment with so they can try it out on other patients and see what the reaction is on certain medications, certain events, how to deal with people. It's kinda like a tug-of-war, like tugging this way trying to get them clothes to fit. I'm backing away and they're bringing me clothes so I could feed them information. They can't do it without me. It's a tug-of-war between the homeless and the staff. The staff doesn't have a job unless there's homeless. The homeless won't have a place to live unless there's staff.

Trust is a thread that is stretched and loosened and wound through the many moments of a relationship, and it can break at various points. When the homeless person and outreach worker have known each other for some time, trust is tied to an investment in the relationship and negotiations over long-term needs. When plans fall through, the relationship can hold up or fall apart, and much will depend on how each party regards the other. The homeless person wonders whether the worker will write him off as a failure or be willing to see him through to the next opportunity. The worker assesses her client's motivation in order to decide how much more energy to expend on his behalf.

In early encounters, though, trust is more of an all-or-nothing proposition. Cynicism and paranoia can produce similar results in the homeless person. Kidd, the young homeless man who we heard from earlier, made the following comments to me about trust:

> Let's face it, I would trust a homeless junkie before I could trust somebody like you. The junkie, you know exactly what he's looking for—his next high, his next fix—and you could be his meal ticket. You're always on your guard. With you, I don't know where you're coming from. You can tell me a whole bunch of shit and I could believe, leaving myself fucked.

Mistrust may come from doubting the worker's (or the researcher's) intentions. It may also come from questioning whether the outsider truly understands or cares about homeless people. Pointing a finger at me in our booth at the Burger King, Kidd challenged me:

> I'd like to get a few of you people together to go out and spend about six nights homeless. Put the billfold away, put the car away, and come out and see what it's like. You go to the overflow shelter some night, you will never want to go there again. It will leave a taste in your mouth you'll never forget. Like eating anchovies. And I don't mean one anchovy, I mean a whole tin of anchovies with no water afterwards.

We should not assume that homeless individuals automatically give workers credit for understanding the homeless experience even when workers give clear demonstrations of doing so. The ineffability or uniqueness that homeless persons ascribe to their experience is no doubt sincerely felt, but it may also be used as a negotiating tool. With it, individuals may signal the pain involved in sacrificing their uniqueness as homeless persons and thus the level of support they will require from outreach workers in compensation for their loss.

Homeless individuals battle their own self-condemnation and fear its confirmation by others. Looking back at his homeless experience, one man talked about the importance of a nonjudgmental approach:

> There are consistent negative vibes working on me. It's a battle. Find out *what* my needs are, not why, not at the beginning. It's none of your business why I'm in this situation. I *am* in this situation. Help me to get out of it. Treat me like a human being. That's the last thing you have when you're homeless, the need for respect in spite of your situation. When you're not given that, you feel rage and contempt.

To treat another like a human being, it is not enough to simply ask the right questions. Respect and dignity, as Michael Ignatieff observes, are a matter of human gestures, not of abstract values. Still, our gestures are motivated in part by our values. Those gestures we make when we think the poor have a right to a decent income will be and look different from those we make when we see the poor as objects of whatever charity we can afford. In the first case, recipients will see our gestures as a transfer of goods between equals; in the second, they will see them as a source of shame for themselves.[3] Peter, who spoke earlier on the nonexperience of homelessness, provides an object lesson in the failure of the judgmental approach. Volunteers from a group called Midnight Run had given him a new pair of boots when he was staying at a shelter. Inside the box, Peter found an inspirational religious message which he interpreted as saying, "We're giving you these boots even though you don't deserve them." His comments to one of the volunteers can help us understand the state of mind of those who must accept charity from others:

> I told her to her face, "You want, I'll take the boots off. I'll walk barefooted. You asked me what I needed, not what I deserved. I don't deserve anything, but I do need boots. If you want to give them to me, give them out of the goodness of your heart. You don't tell a person, 'You don't deserve them.' They wouldn't ask you for them if they didn't need them."

"In a human world," Ignatieff writes, "love and pity must take needs on trust."[4] At the level of basic human needs, including our needs for love and dignity, we must put a stop to reasoning that distinguishes one person's just deserts from another's. Basic needs cannot be determined by merit because determination of merit is tied up with power and privilege and the viewpoints they foster. "Once the rich begin to demand reasons, once they cease to take claims on trust," Ignatieff asks, "what obligations will survive?"[5] If we cannot trust others to know themselves and their needs, we will end by oppressing them.[6]

Homeless individuals evaluate workers' behavior just as workers evaluate that of homeless individuals. The homeless persons I met generally expressed appreciation for the informal and friendly manner of outreach workers. But they were also sensitive to perceived slights or signs that workers were not truly different from other social welfare staff, that they were too busy to provide the individual attention they touted or were unwilling to mix with the homeless:

> They came to me and they really didn't show me enough time. Something always came up: "I can't talk to you now, I gotta give somebody a ride someplace."

> At soup kitchens they don't stand in line and get food. That differentiates them from us. I'd feel more comfortable if they got in line and got food and ate. That would put them at my level. That stigmatism would be taken away.

Homeless persons signal their bargaining power by controlling the time and location of initial encounters. In early negotiations they hold a trump card—the power of rejection. They can simply walk away, or back off and consider what workers have offered them. Workers hold a trump card as well. They can force compliance through involuntary hospitalizations when individuals have mental illnesses that put them in danger on the streets. Workers cannot play this card, though, without violating the guiding principles of outreach. They rarely invoke their power, but they may use it as leverage to persuade homeless street people to come in from the cold.

There are homeless people who want to take the goods— housing, furniture, and money—and run. Clinicians and other mental health workers, looking for therapeutic insight and a therapeutic alliance with the client, are predisposed to see the "loot-takers" as program failures and those who accept treatment as program successes or "hopefuls." And homeless individuals of all categorical stripes talk about the need for emotional support in addition to jobs, housing, and money. Their comments and behavior with trusted staff lend credence to the view of workers that, for many, a positive relationship with another human being is a prerequisite for a successful exit from homelessness. This belief in the importance of human connection simultaneously justifies their work to workers when resources are in short supply and gives homeless persons something to hold on to in their transactions with workers. The quality of homeless persons' relationships with their workers seems to be pivotal in determining whether they take workers' occasional failures to deliver the goods as crushing blows or as temporary setbacks. If they see workers as standing by them, homeless individuals can usually maintain faith in them and in their own chances.

A homeless man named Monk talked about wanting to make contact with staff after living on the streets for twenty years:

> Loneliness is the hardest thing I have to cope with. I've got something to offer ACCESS and I've got something to offer myself. I feel like even America, our society, if they can find that thing, they're going to benefit. I've been alone for a while and a lot of my depression comes from loneliness. There's not many people you can depend on. People you do depend on, you wind up getting hurt, so your tentacles withdraw. You need to support each other. You need to communicate. I'm sick of these streets. I want to be a team member.

Monk saw other programs as forcing treatment down his throat in exchange for tangible goods. He had had enough of that:

> They can't say, "Well, here's a carrot," 'cause I've seen the carrot-stick routine and I've seen more of the stick than I've seen of the carrot and I don't dig it. They can take their carrots and stick them up their ass and I'll be glad to take their stick and beat them with it.

Monk was not negotiating for team membership only. He successfully negotiated for a subsidized apartment in a middle-class high-rise and purchased a good set of furniture with program funds. Perhaps those who meet their expressive needs can best manage their practical needs as well. And perhaps those individuals are also better equipped to match their needs and behavior with mainstream social expectations.

The line between negotiation and manipulation can be hazy at times. Surely, many substance abusers are correctly pegged as being manipulative in requesting goods but balking at treatment that would help them change their lives. Yet if compassion is a sine qua non for workers, it need not always be so for homeless individuals. Much of the outreach teams' ethos was built around a belief in clients' emotional needs; workers can sometimes overlook their own needs for engagement. That some prospective clients seemed not unable but unwilling to fulfill their side of the affective bargain should not blind workers to their own need for human connection and the ways in which this need affects the judgments they make.

Homeless individuals contend with the fact that outreach workers may not be able to deliver all the goods they offer. High caseloads can pinch the quality and quantity of services. Rental-assistance housing is limited, competition is fierce, and the administrative process of gaining approval for housing and moving in can seem endless to the homeless applicant. Those who do not qualify or are put on a long waiting list may have to settle for less comfortable housing than they hoped for. Job training, for those who are interested in and capable of working, does not always lead to a job. A new social network may mean a social club for chronic mental patients, which mentally ill persons often shun because of the stigma associated with mental illness. In some cases, an individual's chief source of social contact after moving into his apartment will be the workers who coaxed him back into the marginal mainstream in the first place.

Homeless persons' often-rosy view of the housed life highlights the deep gulf between their hopes and what workers may be able to deliver. The next speaker is Walter, the alcoholic who lost his wife, his car, and his job, and became homeless. He talked about his plans for his first few days in his own apartment:

> I'm gonna take the first three days to myself. I'm not going anywhere, I'm not doing anything. I'm gonna start getting myself organized and you people are gonna help me find work. I'm gonna get my teeth out. And then I'll be normal again. I want to be free. I don't want any bills, I don't want no problems, no worries, nothing like that. I'm too old for that crap. I had enough problems in my life. I just want to relax now and enjoy.

This may just be wishful thinking on Walter's part. Perhaps he is not as divorced from the reality of housed life as his statement seems to reveal. Walter has a vision of a mainstream life, perhaps harking back to a time before his breakup with his wife, and visions can keep us going without blinding us to practical affairs. The hopelessness that often attends the homeless life is broken by flashes of hope, just as most homeless people have not accepted homelessness as their way of life. Alienation is not necessarily permanent, and it can be a tool for getting through the experience of homelessness rather than an inevitable result of it.[7]

The exit from homelessness is only the last of three marker or crisis points that need to be negotiated with mental health outreach workers on the path from literal homelessness to permanent housing. The first is initial contact with workers. The second is the development of a therapeutic relationship with workers and a decision to accept some of the services they offer. (A corollary to this crisis point is transfer to another clinic for long-term treatment when the outreach team provides only short-term treatment.) The third is the acceptance of housing and the social isolation that often accompanies it. At these crisis points, the homeless person's view of the status he is about to take on stands out in full relief against what he sees as his current status. His fears about what lies ahead will compound the difficulty of making a move. His relationship with the outreach worker simultaneously helps him to negotiate these marker points and carries with it the possibility of a continuing dependence on his worker. It may be that successful incorporation of such transitions functions something like John Strauss's theory of phases of improvement from psychological disorder, where improvement is followed by what appears to be a standstill but is in fact a period of subtle improvement in "self-esteem, stamina, and social skills." This invisible progress strengthens the person's ability to deal with the "discontinuities" of environmental demands.[8]

OUTREACH WORKERS

At the margins, outreach workers are implicitly challenged to drop the heavier armor of professionalism. Traditional mental health assessments, for example, cannot capture the gestalt of the homeless person's life. A clinician with the New Haven outreach project talked about an "extraclinical" understanding in the work. The intake evaluation, which she refers to as a counterpoint to this understanding, would have taken place at the mental health center:

> If somebody walks in for an appointment, the clinician will do an intake evaluation. The clinician never puts in their mind, "What is the experience like, living at Columbus House Shelter?" They lose that from the entire interview, something that's central to the client's life. I think some of the clinical success has been internalizing "What does it mean to be homeless?" You meet the client on a different level. We've truly understood what it means to be homeless. There's different kinds of boundaries in working with these people.

A psychiatrist with the project, who spoke admiringly in the last chapter about the strengths of homeless people, found that he had to learn a new way to assess his homeless patients:

> Homeless people are not as disabled as I thought they were. I look at them with more respect, with admiration about what they're doing and how they're doing it. Talking with homeless people, treating homeless people, has reversed my understanding of psychiatric care. The usual approach is: first medicate the person and then talk to them. In the work we are doing, this has to be reversed. First talk to the patient. First try to engage the patient. First try to address his feelings and his personality, and after you do that, then you can possibly talk about something like medication.

Work at the boundaries calls for surrendering some of the institutional power that adheres to the traditional clinical encounter. In the early stages at least, workers must relinquish control over their potential clients' time. This can be frustrating, especially since workers feel obliged to show up for agreed-upon meetings and homeless individuals may not. This approach is also grossly inefficient by institutional standards. Workers sell their services at unwilling others' pace and erratic schedules and at the sites where they are lucky enough to find them. In New Haven, transactions took place in a buyer's market where workers were under the gun to meet a set quota of clients served regardless of how much time it took to find, negotiate with, and provide services to them. Workers attempted to bring some order into these relationships by training homeless persons to show up for scheduled appointments at convenient meeting places such as the office or an emergency shelter. By doing so, they were extending the long arm of the institution into homeless territory, but they were also instructing their clients in the vital art of negotiating social service bureaucracies.

Relaxing cultural and institutional boundaries does not excuse workers from using sound professional judgment, nor does the use of professional and clinical judgment necessarily imply a loss of contact with the "whole" person. Another psychiatrist with the New Haven ACCESS project observed that unconditional patience with the reluctant client can be an avoidance of true contact. He used the example of a meeting at an emergency shelter between a homeless woman named Andrea and a worker named Jack. Andrea had rejected Jack's plea that she spend the night at the shelter rather than at an abandoned parking garage:

> At times engagement is expressed through setting limits. Andrea worked closely with Jack but refused shelter in the midst of winter temperatures that began to drop to zero. This was a life-threatening situation. After continued attempts to provide shelter, Jack simply but emphatically walked out. Andrea reconsidered the offer and changed her mind. Now she was ready to move into an apartment. To say no, to set limits, to refuse to participate in the ritual of offers that are perceived as rejections and repeated offers that improve the self-image of the generous giver, may mean "being real." There is no engagement without risks.[9]

Traditional classifications and roles begin to lose their outer shape at the margins, but they do not disappear for outreach workers. It may be here, as opposed to the office, that the shape of social division can best be traced. Some workers, for example, saw issues of race and gender as affecting the work, and there were differences along lines of race and gender in how strong they perceived these influences to be. Minority outreach workers were more likely than whites to observe that the significance of color faded at the margins. "Once you're homeless and you're out on the bridge," said one minority worker, "whether you're African American or Caucasian, you both have the same struggle, the same environment." Bill, whom we have heard from before, talked about a seminal encounter for him:

> There was an individual who was on a bench. He was looking at the ground. I said, "Would you like a cup of coffee?" I thought he would have been more receptive, also being a black male.

Bill's offer was rejected coldly. A white man sitting at another bench took the coffee:

> That day was a learning experience. Most of the times it's not a race issue. It's "Can you help me?" Race is such a big issue in this country. Lots of times it's blown out of proportion.

White workers seemed more self-conscious about their color when working with nonwhites than did African American staff when working with whites. Kate, a white clinician, talked about going with two of her black coworkers, Donna and James, to visit the new apartment of Harriet, a black client:

> I was saying [to myself], "I'm the only white person here." Harriet and I have a good relationship, but she made more eye contact with Donna and James than she did with me. And I was in her home. It felt different than when I've interacted with her outside of her home. I was wondering what it was like for her to invite a white person into her home.

Another time, Kate was the only white person in a group that included Harriet and some of her friends:

> I didn't feel uncomfortable. I was wondering how she felt, or how they felt about me being the only white person in the house, and whether or not other white people came into the house.

One wonders whether Kate protests her level of comfort too much, but her comments echo a theme: white workers, especially females, were self-conscious about their membership in a dominant race. They were not always sure that race was an issue for African American homeless persons, but they thought it might be. Sandy, the nurse clinician quoted in chapter 3, commented:

> I wouldn't say it's a prevailing theme. I think it's something you wonder about more than it's actually there: "I wonder if that's going to be an issue working with this person. If I talk to them, how will they react?"

White females worried about coming across as "do-gooders" when working with minority clients, especially black males:

> Why are so many white women in these situations with all these black men? It seems like that's the combination that comes up in the health care system a lot, white women social workers and black men who have all these problems. I think that's set up already in our society.

Sometimes racial discomfort was implied, as in the following comment from another white female:

> I go into the soup kitchens with my own feelings of trying not to present myself as the do-good, authoritative, white social-worker type that's going to come help all the poor people. I think it affects how I present myself to people.

A white male talked about his frustration with African American homeless persons who refused to work with him. He also felt, though, that working through animosity was part of the work:

> They've got reason to resent the way they've been treated. But you have to get beyond that. That's where the "What can I do for you?" comes in: "I'm not offering you any less than I'd offer a white homeless person. You tell me what you think you need and I'll tell you if I can provide it. I understand you've been treated badly, but that's not you and I. You and I are a new thing." I let my deeds speak for themselves.

One white worker attributed a cultural comfort to same-race interactions between minority workers and minority homeless persons:

> I think that approaching the same race is helpful. There's an automatic connection. In the black culture there's black staff and a black client. The client knows that the black staff can relate and know the deprivation of blacks in the past. Their culture is a culture as well as a race. I think they can relate in every way: the types of food they eat, where their family comes from, their ancestors. There's a lot of things in common. The same thing with Hispanics; it's a very close culture.

Black workers, though, rarely talked about cultural heritage as a factor in the work. Perhaps whites felt more at ease than blacks in expressing their sensitivity about racial issues when talking to me, a white interviewer. Perhaps minority staff accustomed to negotiating in a white-dominated society adjusted more easily to racial and cultural differences in their work. Or perhaps the key factor, noted by the speakers above, is that whites working with poor minority individuals were self-conscious about their membership in a dominant group.

Both African American and white workers agreed that there were special issues in working with homeless women. Male outreach workers were wary of working with females, many of whom had been victims of physical and sexual abuse by males. They saw women as having special needs and characteristics:

> Women, they're more receptive to getting services from another woman. Women have been raped, they have been taken advantage of by men time and time again. So they probably find it easier to deal with a woman.

> Women seem to be more standoffish: "I got things under cover, I don't need ACCESS. I could find my own place." Wanting to be in control, more so I think than the men.

Cultural and social forces tremble out from the center to the edges along their fault lines, and I single out issues of race and gender because they are defining, and divisive, elements of mainstream culture. But cultural and professional divisions can also weaken at the boundaries, releasing new energy and new possibilities. If charisma is a gift of grace or a quality that gives a person special influence over others, then the meetings between homeless people and outreach workers are charismatic encounters of a sort. These encounters, taking place at a border of cultural knowledge, are invested with grace and influence for the participants and for distant but curious "onlookers" who are hearing about them. The aura surrounding these meetings is partly a function of a breakdown in the trappings of staff authority and a relative leveling of the playing field. Whose offer can carry the tentative negotiations to a successful conclusion? Whose pathology is at play in failed interactions? If negotiations continue long enough, institutional and cultural influences are likely to give the strategic advantage to the outreach worker, but workers who are honest with themselves will, at odd moments, feel a stirring of doubt.

If the structure of ideas of a society begins to break down at the margins,[10] then the structure of professional relations may break down as well. At the border, normal social buffers that contain our fantasies begin to be sloughed off, surprising us at what their absence reveals about ourselves. Boundary experiences derail our fantasy of a logical progression of events in everyday life. Social life, which seemed reasonably well balanced to us, suddenly looks precarious.[11] The sense of living on the pulse of the moment with the masters of living on that pulse exposes the worker to his other self, the one that wanders, homeless, at the edge of consciousness. And if workers' passion for their work is fueled by their ability to make contact with homeless persons, then their confrontations with those who do not respond to their advances can leave them feeling unmoored and unsettled. The thoughts generated by such encounters go beyond the encounters themselves to make workers (and researchers) question their effectiveness and even the structures that support their social interactions.

Let me illustrate with some encounters with a man named John. Workers found John through his neon yellow sneakers. This was all they could see of him as he lay under half a dozen blankets beneath the Water Street highway bridge one fall morning. They were fairly certain they hadn't met him before and thought it best not to wake him. The next time they came by he was gone, so they looked for his sneakers at the soup kitchens and shelters. A few weeks later they asked some men at the homeless drop-in center if they had seen a man with neon yellow sneakers. "That's John," said one. "He's probably at the library." The workers walked around the public library looking at feet, and found John.

Staff discussed their early speculations about John with the project's attending psychiatrist. Some of these speculations were like those we had about the man behind the door in the basement of the abandoned parking garage. Was John a fugitive from the law? Was he dangerous? He carefully arranged his sleeping quarters as an inmate or a soldier would. These sleeping quarters were his personal signature, which workers spotted under various highway bridges. Outreach workers were engaged with John through their chase after him and their fantasies about him. True interest and curiosity about the other, said the psychiatrist, can pale in the light of our projected images. Could we persuade John, and ourselves, that we had a true interest in him?[12]

I met John sometime later at a downtown soup kitchen. He sat outside of the church parish house, where dinner was served. A worker, Julie, introduced me. She had business to conduct with John, so I drifted off a few paces. She asked him how he was doing. Not well, he said. Had he thought about applying for SSI? "What's the use?" "But you really should think about it," she said. "It could help you get an apartment." John looked at Julie and asked, "How old are you?" In her twenties, she said. "Well, I'm fifty-three and I've made too many mistakes in my life," said John, and he got up and walked away. Afterward, Julie told me she didn't know what to say; she just froze. Crossing the border into John's world, even for a few moments, can bring on such moral paralysis.

My next meeting with John took place at another soup kitchen in the basement of a Roman Catholic church several blocks from downtown. The church was set far back from the street at the end of a broad, untended lawn. No doubt the church's red brick facade, its stained-glass windows, and its remoteness from the road had once helped worshipers pass from the worldliness of the sidewalk to the piety of the sanctuary. In the fall of 1994, though, its remoteness gave it a forbidding appearance. The front steps were almost out of earshot of the few passersby on the sidewalk. The parking lot on the right was obscured by bushes and the narrow alleyway on the left that led to the soup kitchen stretched away into shadow. The church was about to close down. Its original Italian parishioners had long since moved to East Haven and its mostly Latino replacements had dwindled in number and income. The soup kitchen was doomed.

I parked on the street and walked in by the alleyway. A woman was taking names for an "unduplicated" count for the food-bank allotment. John sat at the far end of a community room filled with wooden tables in long parallel rows. I walked to the back with my coffee for a prop. Peter, a buddy of John's from the bridge, was sitting on the other side of the table and a couple of seats down, reading a paperback book and listening to a transistor radio. The first time I met Peter, he burst out laughing from time to time or talked out loud, either to himself or to the radio or to internal voices. Or perhaps he did these things because he was not really alone: I, this stranger, was sitting nearby, and he was telling me to keep my distance.

I sat down on Peter's side of the table, diagonally across from John, who did not acknowledge me. I waited.

"Hello, John. Do you remember me?"

He scowled. "Yes, I do."

"How're you doing?"

"You asked the question, you already know the answer."
I paused. "How's lunch here?"
"Good."
I paused, longer. "Have the outreach workers been able to help you at all? Like with housing?"
"You asked the question, you already know the answer."
And John got up and walked away. Looking to my right, I saw the hint of a smile on Peter's face.

Clinicians who have spent time with John might recognize in this brief exchange signs of his depression and feelings of worthlessness. John is white. He grew up in a large, poor family in a rural area near Cincinnati. He left home at seventeen to join the army, on the heels of a scandal involving himself and his much younger girlfriend. After getting an honorable discharge in the early 1960s, John drifted south and drank himself out of one menial job after another. In 1991, he came to the New Haven area and stayed with his brother for a few months, but was asked to leave because of his drinking. John had lived under a highway bridge for about a year with Peter and a couple of other men who were his only social contacts.

John's statement—"You asked the question, you already know the answer"—may mean "You're part of that homeless project, so you already know a lot about me." But it may also reflect his refusal to be understood too easily: "You think you know the answer before you ask the question. But you don't know me, or the answer, or even what questions to ask." Or "People like you never ask questions of people like me unless you already know the answer." The answer being, of course, that if you're eating in a soup kitchen you can't be doing *too* well.

Students of "symbolic interaction" would say that my difficulty in making contact with John was that we lacked a shared world of meaning. Meaning, in symbolic interaction theory, is a social product emerging from social interactions. Even before these interactions take place, however, most of us share an understanding of how to act in social situations and what to expect of others.[13] Our knowledge of common meanings and our abil-

ity to engage in social interactions come not only from our experience as social veterans, but also from our ability to imaginatively put ourselves in someone else's shoes.[14] Without a shared
sense of meaning, communication becomes impossible. When
one of the parties to the social interaction fails to acknowledge
or act upon the implications of commonly held meanings, he
places in jeopardy the other's sense of "intersubjective reality."[15]

John has lost or chosen not to use the symbols of everyday
interaction. The only way to get to know him is to learn to understand his world and the meanings he attaches to it. John's all-
purpose curse ("You asked the question, you already know the
answer") might translate as follows: "We share nothing, you and
I, and I do not care to pretend that we do." Such a response, sig-
naling defeat and despair, is also a power play. With a few words
that struck at the unequal relationship implied in my encounter
with him, John was able to keep the world at bay once again and
remain at home in his otherness, his sense that the border between him and the world was fixed and forever closed. Or was
this encounter a rejection only of my terms and an invitation on
his? "Can you tolerate my world? Can you bear the discomfort
of sitting with me? Will you pass the test and come back to be
tested again?"

Students of what Herbert Garfinkel calls "ethnomethodology" might say that my encounter with John exposes some of
the taken-for-granted, invisible rules and expectations of everyday life.[16] In social interaction, two parties agree to accept certain signals as invitations to a dance whose first steps are taken
with the invitation itself. These signals function as "background
expectancies." For us to become consciously aware of these
expectations, we must "either be a stranger to the 'life as usual'
character of everyday scenes or become estranged from them."[17]
Or, as Erving Goffman put it, we must look to "extraordinary
situations where the student can stumble into awareness."[18]

Homeless encounters can constitute such extraordinary situations. When the object of the worker's or researcher's attention
declines his offer, the fluid code that guides the steps of the

dance no longer applies and the music stops abruptly. The unconscious code is made conscious and is seen as a cultural artifact with no intrinsic meaning. Adding the element of power to my brief meeting with John, one might say that the lie of equity in the social encounter is unmasked to reveal the dominance that one party normally exercises. And this exposure is never more bald than in meetings at the margins.

Not all mentally ill homeless persons "incommunicate" so aggressively as John. Many are articulate in ways that move or enlighten us. They may enlighten us most, however, when they talk about the sense of alienation that John embodies. John himself is probably more unable than unwilling to participate in conventional social interactions. But if we must not forget the clinical pathology of mentally ill homeless persons, then a fair analysis of boundary transactions must also take into account the institutional pathology exhibited by the "double-bound" worker who must simultaneously provide personal care to unique individuals and process those individuals through social service bureaucracies.

At the border, secret wishes and impulses may assert themselves. Imaginative entry into damaged lives forces workers to run a gamut of emotions. The seduction of danger and love for a fellow human being can cause workers to detonate the land mines of bureaucracy. Clinical distance can become a vanishing perspective. Workers use their own money when they can't wait for petty cash, their own cars when agency vehicles are not available. These are peccadilloes, perhaps not violations at all from where the worker stands. But workers may be tempted to go further, leaving open the back door of the agency van on a cold night when the homeless person refuses to go to the shelter. This flies in the face of bureaucratic if not clinical propriety, and workers risk their livelihoods by giving in to such humanistic impulses. Still, the chance of detection is small, the homeless person is likely to keep the secret, and such acts are reasonable responses to bad weather and bad rules. But less experienced workers may lose sight of expediency and indulge themselves in savior fantasies, losing all professional objectivity and thereby the ability to help their clients over the long haul.

There are less humanistic impulses as well. The other side of compassion is revulsion at physical and moral filthiness, which thoughts and sightings of homeless persons can invoke.[19] Fear of contamination, of infection, of losing one's moral and psychic bearings, perhaps even of dissolution and death, are triggered by the stranger's violation of our cultural island. Face-to-face with the other, we experience contrary extremes of compassion and disgust, curiosity and flight. Moral disorder may also strike from within—as a sudden realization of one's power to give or take services, or as a temptation to dangle the carrot of services, not to entice the individual into treatment but simply for the sake of dangling. Homeless encounters are at once morally dangerous, exciting, seductive, and charismatic for the outreach worker.

The freedom of outreach work leaves workers exposed to moral uncertainty and impulses that are contained indoors. But along with a Pandora's box of forbidden impulses comes a countervailing structure that workers carry with them when they leave the office. The staff role orients and clothes workers, giving them work to do and a sense of style with which to carry it off. It situates them in an internal bureaucratic time and space that qualifies the influence of street time and street space. Work at the boundaries chips away at professional roles but does not dislodge them.

More than any other factor, it is the power to distribute services and resources, not the cloak of officialdom or an insinuation of the dominant culture into the homeless encounter, that protects the worker from confusion or even moral terror. The fact that workers have services to dispense structures their interactions with homeless persons and creates unequal power relationships. Of course, the goal of providing services is to give the homeless person a chance at a better life. If offering help also helps workers to manage their own feelings and impulses, then who would quibble? After all, there is more to dealing with homelessness than empathy. Hunger strikes in the belly, and blankets, not understanding, take the edge off the chill under a highway bridge. Homeless people and outreach workers may be sizing each other up for the next step in the social transaction, but homeless people hope to purchase tangible goods with their cooperation and outreach workers hope to justify their work. Taxpayers, even those most sympathetic to the plight of the poor, do not pay for a shared sense of meaning but for services that improve people's lives in measurable ways. John went from sleeping under highway bridges to living in his own apartment, from having no income to receiving support from federal entitlement programs, and from getting no mental health treatment to getting some. Still, the expressive and instrumental domains of boundary encounters are intertwined. John will lock himself in his apartment for weeks at a time unless his worker comes to spend time with him. For many, human contact and trust are preconditions for being able to accept tangible help such as housing. Once they are housed, their relationships with workers may be as important as tangible goods for keeping them from becoming homeless again.

Workers talked about both the practical and the emotional needs of homeless persons. Instrumental needs can be as basic as a cup of coffee and a sandwich or a birth certificate and a Social Security card. They can be as substantial as housing. Meeting the latter may involve persuading individuals that they deserve their own place, then helping them obtain an income and rent support, and then finding sympathetic landlords who will offer them safe apartments at a price they can afford. Workers talked about the need for "transitional" housing as a step between homelessness and permanent housing, "for people who need a period of time to ease back into housing, a place without a lease where you don't have to get a phone and furniture and all the cooking utensils and pay your utilities." It is not just a matter of getting used to living in a home and having the responsibilities of mainstream life, but of learning or relearning the skills of housed life. Ed, who became John's primary worker, talked about moving him and his buddies from the bridge into their own apartments:

> We take him from under the bridge and put him into a house. Going through that transition, it's a struggle for him. If he had a transitional house, that would help out a lot. While they're in the house we would be able to do some training and teach everyday skills. They were living under a bridge without water, no soap. You want to change your clothes, wash your clothes, take care of yourself. A transition back into the community.

Workers spend much of their time negotiating tangible services for homeless persons, but feel that human contact and caring are essential elements in both their negotiations with individuals and the unwritten contracts that come out of those negotiations. One clinician said that, for some clients, the worker is the first nurturing adult they have ever known. Another said, "We've become a replacement family." There is a danger in replacing natural family with "program family," yet at times workers can function as transitional rather than replacement family members. Human contact restored and solidified, some individuals are able to renew contact with their families of origin.

Compassion and understanding make trust possible, workers think, and trust helps people reestablish their place in the mainstream community. The first speaker refers to Monk, who spoke earlier about wanting to be a "team member":

> People say they want housing, but I think they really do want contact with people and haven't had it for quite a while, or have only had it with other people who are down-and-out. Monk talks about being around these "degenerates" all the time. That's how he sees it, living in a society of outcasts. To have a link or contact with people outside of that world is really important.
>
> A relationship with someone they know cares about them—with that maybe things are possible. Without that trust they'll stay under the bridge. They need to believe in something or someone.

The skeptic might argue that workers exaggerate their expressive function because their practical function fails to satisfy either their own needs to reach out to alienated individuals or their clients' needs for housing and money. Exaggerated or not, workers' belief in the efficacy of personal contact helps them to manage the despair of witnessing deep poverty they cannot dispel, the frequent rejection of services they can offer, and the cultural gap between them and their clients. Indeed, to insist on a separation of instrumental and expressive needs may be the true delusion. Homeless people, with the exception of a few that may have been permanently numbed by years on the streets or untreated mental illness, find openings in time to make plans, to dream, and to project an image of themselves into a better future.[20] Practical and emotional needs, as Sandy argues, go together:

> The sooner you can create something for people to do in the community that gives them a sense of purpose and a sense of belonging to the greater society, the better. The longer that time lapse, the harder it is for people to get back on their feet. If these guys want to work, even though they look shitty because they live under the bridge, if that's what they want to do and they could get there a couple of times a week, maybe that would be a big boost to them.

The staff role, as Sandy notes, can also be a barrier in boundary transactions, and thus a barrier to helping people move out of homelessness:

> We put up boundaries between ourselves and patients. In some ways that's useful to us to be able to continue giving care to people, but it also isolates us from really knowing who people are. In what ways are we like them? In what ways are we not like them? You have to insulate yourself to some degree, but that also serves to alienate people: "I could pull some strings and do something here or I could chose not to." That's there before that person knows it. Once you establish that you're any kind of professional, that this person could need your services, there's a hierarchy. They're the needy one and you're the one who has the power to provide or not provide.

Still, even with caveats, street work is different from office work. Sandy continued:

There's a freedom outside. You can be in the community seeing someone and you're free to be the person that you are. There's no supervisor looking over your shoulder. You have some leeway to decide how you want to present yourself. It's in a common territory. That person can walk away, you could walk away. That openness is there, and just by talking there's a choice that's mutual. In an office setting the person comes and agrees to be compliant with treatment. On the street, even though one can do something for the other, there's an assumed agreement that they'll talk, even if it's just for that moment. There's something established that isn't present in an institutional setting.

Faith in the "specialness" of outreach work helps to carry workers not only through frequent failures to make contact, but through the dichotomy of street work and people-processing that shapes their work and their clients' futures.

THE PRICE OF HELP

Homeless encounters provide an occasion for negotiations and transactions over expressive and instrumental goods, and there is a price to be paid for goods received in that way. The immediate price that homeless individuals pay is their privacy. Whether they agree to participate in a research project, accept medical or mental health treatment, or simply apply for local General Assistance, they will have to answer many questions they can avoid on the streets. For many of us, the official collection of personal information is occasional. The data bank is already full of us and requires only updating from time to time. We also have some positive associations with giving information (though alloyed by the sense of violation that comes from knowing that strangers can learn so much about us with a keystroke): information helps us to get jobs, mortgages, loans, and credit cards. But for the marginal person, the act of surrendering personal information is stigmatizing in itself, carrying associations of poverty, disability, and dependence rather than consumption.

A second price is that of negative or ambiguous identity. If, as David Snow and Leon Anderson suggest, many homeless individuals create alternate ways of life with alternate identities,[21] then, having constructed these identities, they may be wary of making another transition. The thought of giving up one's homeless identity, patched and pasted together though it may be, for another, of giving up homeless acquaintances for the isolation of apartment living, raises doubts about self-worth that can be pushed down more easily in the day-to-day foraging for subsistence.[22] One young woman who had lived on the streets talked about compatriots who had spent more time there than she:

> When you're older and you've been on the street for a while you're afraid to get off. You feel like you're never going to be normal again. Can you live your life with a job and have a normal apartment and eat normal meals and do normal things? People take that for granted. They have a home to go to every night and a husband or wife or kids that they play with. Then they have dinner and they go to bed and get up in the morning, and have their morning coffee and read the *Register* [a New Haven daily newspaper], and go to work in their nice car and hold their job all day and have lunch and go home and do it all over again.

The housed life that this woman hesitates to accept is almost as stereotyped as the mainstream view of homelessness. But those whose lives have been disrupted for a brief spell may also idealize their now-endangered routines and comforts.

For some who are homeless, the fear of being housed may be a fear of giving up the excitement of living on the pulse of the moment:

> Homeless people and addicts love chaos. They don't know how to live normal lives. "Well, what am I gonna do when I get clean? Jog?" It's not that they're putting down people who jog, it's just that, "God I've been through so much. Can I ever live like a normal person?"

For others, the routine of going from shelter to soup kitchen to waiting for the library to open is a numbing existence, but it is known. Accepting help means accepting the threat as well as the promise of a new way of life. Depending on the length of time the person has spent homeless and the number of bridges he has burned, this new way may be familiar or it may be lost to memory.[23]

The to-be-housed person's new identity may be that of a mental patient. "You mean to tell me I have to be crazy to get help?" one individual asked an outreach worker. "Why couldn't I just be homeless?" asked another. The stigma does not have to be mental illness, though, and outreach workers are not the only bearers of the double-edged sword of services and tainted identity. The price of self-esteem can come with assistance as basic as food stamps, and it is paid by the poor in general. For one man, it was not food stamps or General Assistance alone that shamed him, but their association with a loss of control during a time when he was homeless and using drugs. His sense of violation by the welfare system and his self-loathing were of a piece:

> You feel like less of a man, like you shouldn't be getting these things. When I hand the food stamps, I pay a price. I'm sending myself a message. You shouldn't have to give these little pieces of paper so everyone can know you're getting charity. A lot of it was my own doing, but even so . . . "Feed me, clothe me, house me, I'm finished." You give up.

Looking back at his own homeless life and his progress through social service systems, this man made the point that the recipient's self-esteem and sense of autonomy are, in part, functions of whether there are special requirements for receiving the service and of whether there is a one-to-one relationship with a service provider:

> There are homeless people who feel independent despite the fact that they're being fed at a soup kitchen, being housed in a shelter, getting entitlements: "I'm my own man. I'm doing my own thing. I'm making the decisions. I choose to be at a shelter, I choose to be at a soup kitchen." But when you get connected to a case manager, there's a dependency that's created on another

person because of the personal relationship that forms with the person, as opposed to going to soup kitchens [where] there's no *one* person that's helping you.

In the absence of program requirements, you do not have to please anyone and you are not a "client." In the soup kitchen, for example, food is a right, not a privilege. Show up, don't threaten or hit anyone, and they have to serve you. The fine print on the contract with the worker, though, states that the individual will become known as a client and processed through social service bureaucracies.

Homeless persons may feel they have to please workers in order to receive the goods that workers offer. The man who spoke just above had seen this side as well:

> The way a homeless person will talk to a person that's a provider of services as opposed to another homeless person or a person on the street—they know there's something you can give them, so they're a little more courteous when they talk to you. They want something, so they're a little kinder. Their mannerisms change. When you're providing a service to them they have a reason to play the role.

Sandy talked about the expectations of "getting better" that are built into the worker-client relationship:

> You [can] focus on the "if": "If you meet the criteria, or if you do *x, y, z,* I can possibly do this." Or you can emphasize the possibilities without the other person's behavior or situation being what you're looking at. You're always free to do that. You see them for who they are, not for what they could be if you changed them. "If they acted differently then they could have these things . . ."—that's pretty loaded. Who knows if that person wants to change? That whole idea of being something different than who they are already . . .

One worker felt that outreach workers challenged the homeless individual's "ingrained self-image." The message from society is "You are undeserving," but suddenly workers are saying the opposite: "You're deserving. We want to help you. You should have this and you can have this." Without question, this new message is a more positive one for the homeless person to hear, but it can be confusing as well. This same worker commented on the importance of not assuming that all individuals will want to relinquish the contingent life of homelessness:

> We are so wrapped up in being the helpers [and] the assumption that people will want what we have. They don't always, or not at that particular moment, or not that week. "Why didn't they want what I had to offer? They need it." But here I am, this homeless person, I live my life the way I live it day by day, surviving and getting through, and here's this person comes along assuming I need help. Maybe my perception is that nothing needs to change.

Workers feel that homeless persons give up some of their freedom in asking for help and taking on the responsibilities of "socializing more, attending appointments, and paying bills." The next two speakers, with different perspectives and sympathies, commented on the freedom of a lack of mainstream structures and responsibilities:

> After being out there and doing things the way they've been, they're giving up their freedom to live any way that they want to live and not comply with any type of rules or structure or any environment that has all these stipulations on them. The responsibility part of it is something they don't like.

> They've never had to ask for help before. They think they're doing fine, and you come along and tell them they're not doing fine. Some of them are embarrassed by the way they're living, but they don't want you to feel their embarrassment. They got along fine without a birth certificate or whatever and now they have to get it to get services. Some of them will do without.

Homeless individuals face the challenge of success and the fear of failure both subjectively and in relation to their workers. Outreach workers agree that their clients may carry around an "unspoken feeling of having to succeed," and they realize that their own desire to see their clients make it influences this feeling. Homeless persons sometimes pay the price of partial success when workers become judgmental over their partial failure. A senior clinician was dismayed at workers' anger toward a man named Jeff who had made headway in his mental health treatment but relapsed with his addiction. She felt that workers were tougher on him than they were on others with whom they had been unable to make any connection at all. "Why are we judging Jeff so harshly?" she asked them. One answer was "Well, he's asking for help." She talked about this attitude:

> It's the peril of partial success. We impose restrictions on him because he's asking for help. The other people we're working with that don't ask for help, don't want to get clean, don't want to have clinical treatment—we don't have to impose limits on these clients. I think it's people's frustrations and how difficult it is to work with somebody who's improving and [then] falls down. The guy is asking for services. People get excited, they get invested personally and they feel as though the person has made an implicit promise to them and broken it and betrayed them. Somebody who just totally screws up, they didn't have that same investment in the sense of promise from this guy who has reneged on the agreement.

Jacqueline Wiseman wrote that workers' offer of help or withdrawal of compassion is related to the route by which homeless individuals come to their present condition. If workers see the client's situation as "not his own fault," they will have more sympathy for him. Given this starting point, workers then expect compliant behavior from their clients. The social workers whom Wiseman observed regarded their alcoholic clients as manipulators if they returned to drinking after having received housing, medical care, or other goods. Manipulation, they seemed to feel, should be the prerogative of helpers alone.[24] John Gusfield describes three types of deviants and their fate in the hands of the helping professions. The "repentant" deviant knows and is willing to declare that he is deviant. The "dominated" deviant does not acknowledge his deviance, but does not attack the normative position espoused by helpers. The third type of deviant is an enemy to the normative order and directly flouts its values.[25] Jeff displayed behavior characteristic of the first and second, salvageable, groups. He was compliant with his mental health treatment and showed appreciation to staff for their efforts. He did not deny his need for drug treatment, but he did not embrace it. Yet staff seemed to regard Jeff's return to drug use as a direct affront, placing him in the third, unsalvageable group, even if, in their calmer moments, they would have described his addiction as a disease.

So the move into the housed world is psychological as well as physical. One worker talked about the "invisibility" of homelessness and the "visibility" of work, home, and responsibility that comes with mainstream life. Another saw the mainstream sense of time as a barrier:

> Some people don't play the game well of paying bills and doing all the things you have to do to be a good citizen. They never learned how. They haven't had a role model to do that; it never worked for them. They have to pay bills on time and they're not very good about time. They never did anything on time. These things become like a trap to them. It's a set-up to fail.

One could argue that many homeless persons are more skilled at using time than middle-class persons whose time is regulated for rather than by them. Still, this worker is right about the new beat of time her clients will be moving to when they take up residence in their apartments and have to pay bills, do the shopping, and engage in other activities that go with being domiciled.

The adjustment to having and being around material possessions is psychological and physical as well. A worker, referring to a client named Richard, talks about the first type of adjustment, and a homeless man talks about the second:

> It's easy to lose perspective on how simple things can be tasks for people who haven't done something for a long time. What seems easy is monumental to them. Richard says, "I don't want too many things. I have a bed and a chest and that's enough 'cause I don't know what I'd do with these other things." Even owning

possessions feels like a burden to him. What does he do with them? He feels some kind of relationship has to exist with these things. They become responsibilities to him.

When you get in that home you have to make another adjustment. I was homeless for a long time. I was sleeping in a vacant house on Winchester Avenue on the floor. And right now, today, I sleep on the floor a lot. It's hard for me to sleep in a bed. Believe it or not, it's hard for me to sleep in a bed.

It may simply be a matter of time for people to adjust to these changes if other aspects of their housed life fall into place. But homeless people must negotiate more treacherous terrain. Their social networks may be thin by normal standards, but they do have contact with their homeless peers. This changes dramatically when they move into their own apartments. Their new-found social isolation is a larger and longer-term problem for them than that of adjusting to sleeping in a bed. Outreach workers who have scrambled to find apartments for homeless individuals may feel uneasy about their clients' future, as do the homeless individuals themselves. "I think it's the worst thing in the world sometimes for a person to have their own place, to live alone, have solitude, have the temptation of everything that could come with that," said one homeless person with a history of substance abuse. One worker noted the difference between having to think about survival twenty-four hours a day but being part of a larger homeless community, and of living alone in one's apartment: "When they shut their door in their apartment, they really have to confront how isolated they are."

Workers, as I mentioned earlier, saw "transitional" housing as one partial solution to this dilemma, and a number of forms of "supported" and "independent" housing have been studied.[26] But the sea change from homelessness to being housed is not one that admits of a simple programmatic solution. Paul Koegel writes that many service providers have difficulty understanding why homeless individuals may be reluctant to accept housing. An insider's view teaches the price of such a choice. Apartments and residential programs may be dead ends of routine and dependence for individuals who have survived outside. "Home-lessness," he writes, "carries significant costs, but at least leaves one's sense of autonomy and self-determination intact, and does not lock one into a patient identity."[27] The housed life can be an alien world, especially for long-term homeless individuals. For some, the fear of becoming housed and of then losing their apartments because of poverty or personal disability or bad luck can keep them on the street.

Outreach workers try to encourage their clients to return to the mainstream, but the idea that homeless persons are returning to any niche that society has kept open for them may be fanciful.[28] The thought that housing may bring with it a second-class citizenship haunts both parties. Here, after arriving at the mainland, the homeless person's status as a poor immigrant becomes most apparent. The barrenness of the landscape that stretches before him cannot be ignored. His plot is narrow, and the few opportunities he can see for himself outside his plot are few, distant, and forbidding.

SOCIAL IMAGINATION

There are profound differences between the experiences of homeless and comfortably housed people, and strong barriers to mutual understanding. When I asked Kidd what it was like to be homeless, he shot back at me, "What's it like to be a cup of coffee?" He continued:

> You're a virgin, you have sex and somebody explains it to you. Doing it and then trying to explain it to somebody who's never done it . . . You understand what I'm talking about?

The ineffable is that which cannot be communicated. It is incommensurable with everyday reality and cannot be spoken of easily in the thick tongue of everyday language. The ineffable has a quality of "in-itself-ness" that defies comparison. Even to speak of it is almost to commit sacrilege. Of course the claim of ineffability, as Walter Kauffman observes, may simply expose the speaker's inability to communicate or the listener's inability to ask the right questions, or both. The poet who claims ineffability as an excuse for not exploring, in words, the experience his words have led us to is no poet at all.[29] But even Shakespeare must have paused at King Lear's cliff. And perhaps part of the play's message is that we can all be victims of disaster at the margins of the known world if we are unable to talk about it—if, as Joyce Carol Oates has written, we act "as if the measure of sanity were the capacity to assimilate horrors without comment."[30] If there are core or fringe experiences that are ineffable, they may be more or less so depending on the relationship of speaker to listener. Giving an approximate rendering of a traumatic experience in words and actions may be a compromise we have to make to retrieve our full humanity from disaster. Such a compromise may even call on a deeper and broader imagination than that evoked by the "in-itself-ness" of the unspeakable.

Ineffability, in addition to implying an inability to convey one's deepest feelings and experiences, seems to imply the other's willingness but inability to understand. Homeless people do not necessarily assume that people are willing to hear them out, and they aren't always sure they want to try to explain themselves. My question to one informant—"Suppose you had an auditorium full of people who had never been homeless and you could say anything you wanted to about being homeless. What would you tell them?"—revealed to this man my basic misunderstanding of the chasm between the two groups:

> I wouldn't waste my time. First of all, if you finally did get an audience they would not be there of their own free will. So whatever you say would go in one ear and out the other. As far as telling them, I would basically rely on their questions. You can't sit down and say, "Here until seven-thirty and then staying on the Green." That doesn't mean anything unless there is a desire for them to learn.

When we think of homeless people as having been hammered and displaced by economic catastrophe and we say that they live outside the edges of society, we may wonder whether they can find a common world of meaning with those who live within it. Trauma, as Kai Erikson has written, can create the most improbable of social groups, a community of people who have withdrawn into themselves but who share a "spiritual kinship" by which "estrangement becomes the basis for communality, as if persons without homes or citizenship or any other niche in the larger order of things were invited to gather in a quarter set aside for the disenfranchised, a ghetto for the unattached."[31] Others, writing about the importance of finding meaning in disaster, have argued that survivors can use the wisdom they earned from those events to enrich our understanding of disaster. The public's acknowledgment of their suffering may then help them to rebuild their lives and gain a sense that they can right a world gone wrong.[32] In my interviews with homeless people, I was taken by the eloquence of those who, given their deficits in education, their lack of opportunity to be heard, and the "ineffability" they often impute to their experience, have every reason to be struck dumb by what has befallen them. If such a community exists in the negative sense, then perhaps these individuals can teach the meaning of their struggle to others.[33] Their testimony might reveal that the homeless person's survival strengths can find a niche within the American values of independence and self-reliance and thus help to dispel the image of homeless persons as misfits. In doing so, homeless persons may also help us, as Jim Baumohl has observed, to rediscover the meanings of "citizenship" and participation in civic life.[34]

Boundary encounters, more than most social interactions, are focal points where appearance and reality often clash. The homeless man who appears tame at a social club, with the dull, medicated glaze of a chronic mental patient, may appear angry and menacing when standing outside a shelter at nightfall in the dead of winter. Of course, he may *be* angry standing out in the cold and glazed in the warmth of the social club. But the appearance of ferocity on the street may also be intentional, the homeless person's mask for the mean streets of the city. How do workers convey to those who have lost contact with society that there is a better life for them? Do workers always believe that this is so? Or do they suspect that some individuals have been so severely damaged as to be beyond the help of housing and money, and incapable of normal human relationships? And how do workers explain themselves to themselves when the part of them that wants to disappear, to become invisible, to forgo the responsibilities of mainstream life, appears at their side in the midst of their homeless encounters?

The transactions of homeless persons and outreach workers are rich in fantasy, and potentially destructive because of this. The next step beyond fantasy is what I propose to call "social imagination."[35] Social imagination starts with an ability to cross cultural barriers by drawing upon our own experiences and imaginatively inserting ourselves into the situation of others. Having taken this leap, social imagination then involves working with the other to achieve certain negotiated goals. By this definition and in this context, fantasy and the projection of our desires and fears onto others are debased forms of imagination that keep others at bay and protect us from having to acknowledge our frightening kinship with and difference from them.

Social imagination can be compared to the professional practice of empathy, a concept that has been gaining attention in the field of medicine.[36] It is this, but it also involves a commitment to helping others gain access to resources and to a sense of rights and belonging as community members and citizens. The main, though not the sole burden, of responsibility for the use of social imagination in the encounters described in this report falls on outreach workers. Homeless persons, after all, are entitled to a dose of skepticism about workers. Workers must enter into imaginative sympathy with the wounded without incurring permanent damage to themselves. They must then help the wounded to develop strategies across a broad spectrum of instrumental and expressive needs.

John Guare's play *Six Degrees of Separation,* a satire on the upper middle class and chic liberalism, also provides a brilliant illustration of how social fantasy falls short of social imagination. Guare's title refers to the boundary-smashing notion that only six people separate us from any other person on earth. Find the right six people, for example, and a Manhattan socialite "knows" a dirt-poor native in an Amazonian jungle. In Guare's play, Paul, a homeless street hustler, takes on an alternate identity as Sidney Poitier's son. (Paul is never characterized as homeless, but it is clear that he has no permanent abode and lives by his wits on the street.) He learns about the art dealers Flan and Ouisa Kittredge from a friend of the Kittredges' children whom he has hustled. One evening he knocks frantically on the door of the Kittredges' apartment claiming he has just been mugged. He explains that he got the Kittredges' address from their children, his classmates at Harvard.

Paul's wound is slight. He recovers and charms the Kittredges with his story of life as Sidney Poitier's son. He charms them, too, with his discourse on the failure of imagination in twentieth-century life. "The imagination," he contends, "is the passport that we create to help take us into the real world." Paul sticks the irony of his theme to the Kittredges, whose imagination is strong enough to buy his false story but too weak to see the dispossessed person who wants desperately to belong to their world. Eventually, Paul's ruse is exposed, but Ouisa, his alternate mother, shifts her fantasy of knowing the brilliant son of Sidney Poitier to that of grooming a street genius for success in her world. At the end of the play, Paul is arrested for larceny, the falseness of the Kittredges marriage is exposed as thoroughly as that of Paul's relationship to Sidney Poitier, and Ouisa strikes out on her own.[37]

Now, one would not want a street hustler to stand for homeless people in general. And one would not want a superficial couple like the Kittredges to stand for the pioneers we call outreach workers (although we might let them stand for the general public in its relationship to homeless people). But beneath the surface of his satire on the ignorant rich, Guare draws a portrait of a failure of social imagination. Ouisa falls in love with her own image of life on the streets. Her savior fantasies stem from a need to save her own life—an acceptable starting point if she could acknowledge it as such. But Ouisa is alienated from herself and her own world and thus cannot know Paul or his world. She walks away from her empty life into another empty life like a middle-aged Huck Finn turning his back on society and calling it freedom. She is the victim of her own lack of imagination, and she has failed to help Paul, who is trapped in his poverty and his fantasy of making it in Ouisa's world. Both parties have reached a border where the structure of ideas that sustained their lives can reach no further. Neither has been able to make true contact with the other.

Still, social imagination must grow from the rich soil of our own experience. It is in face-to-face confrontations with homeless individuals that workers develop a broader approach to their work, one that weds clinical understanding and human sympathy to tangible goods. But workers and students of homeless encounters must go further. They must ask the question, Whose imagination, and what reality? What, after all, keeps social imagination from being the kind of insulated cultural vision that Guare exposes in the Kittredges? The compassion that workers offer on the streets may strike some homeless persons as so much bleeding-heart liberalism and personal guilt—better than the scorn of the public at large, maybe, but a far cry from true understanding. Jacqueline Wiseman suggests that our expectation of the homeless person's return to the mainstream is a middleclass concept that has little relevance to people who are coping with day-to-day life in an alien world.[38] Beyond any specific interventions or approaches, social imagination needs to incorporate what social scientists call reflexivity, the ability to ask questions outside of as well as through our professional framework and training.[39] It is a hard thing to ask those whose work requires a deep personal commitment to simultaneously question the purpose of what seems to be a self-evident good. But workers, even with the best and most humanitarian intentions, are influenced by ideologies that reflect their own interests. While focusing on the objects of their help, workers must also examine the interests and influences they carry with them into the field. They must make problematic their own grounds, including their own social imaginations. Failing to do this, they may create new and more subtle barriers for those whom they wish to help.

5

The Business of Homelessness

There is much to be said for public bureaucracies. They have the human and financial resources to initiate change, even if they simultaneously resist change. They can be havens of mediocrity, but they can also attract talented staff who set high standards for themselves and their organizations. The federal government has been the last bastion of support for those who cannot compete in the marketplace, and this support is often delivered through public agencies that deliver social services on a large scale to large groups of people.[1] Even the philosophy of individual care may be given its widest audience through bureaucratic processes. A federal interagency task force, building upon a decade of services and research financed with public funds, recommended federal funding for the ACCESS project.[2]

State and local bureaucracies may take leadership on public policy issues. In Connecticut, senior administrators from the state mental health funding authority championed the cause of mentally ill homeless persons. They engineered successful funding proposals for outreach, case management, and housing programs, and a statewide policy to give homeless individuals equal priority for residential programs that had previously been reserved for patients being discharged from state psychiatric hospitals. In New Haven, the local mental health authority worked with the state authority to develop new homelessness programs for its service area.

Bureaucracy provides the means for starting and stopping efforts to address social problems and for making decisions about who will receive what services. These decisions are not based on mere rational calculation of need. They are social and political in nature and are funneled through administrative mechanisms for determining need and response to need. Such mechanisms make possible the mobilization of large-scale relief efforts, but they also distance us from the lives of unique individuals.[3] Michael Ignatieff writes that the modern welfare state's admirable goal of supplying people with basic needs so they can be free to "choose the good" is implemented by administrators who, in making categorical decisions about the lives of strangers, simultaneously limit individual freedom.[4]

Public social service bureaucracies may simultaneously promote and stifle innovation. A case example is systems integration—the attempt to coordinate systems of care such as health, mental health, housing, income support, and employment in order to improve human services. (The notion that a group of local service agencies represent a "system" of care because they serve the same clientele often represents wishful thinking, but use of the term is so widespread that writers on this topic are hard-pressed to field a team without using it.) Systems integration theory first became popular during the 1960s and 1970s, when the rapid growth of human service programs, coupled with such factors as deinstitutionalization—the massive discharge of chronic mentally ill persons from state hospitals—led to increasing complexity and fragmentation of service programs and often rendered services inaccessible to potential clients.[5] Systems integration was proposed as a method of coordinating services by creating policy and programmatic linkages within and across disciplinary systems of care. From a public financing perspective, systems integration held out the promise of increasing the efficiency and economy of existing services[6] and has at times been offered as an alternative to simply expanding services.

Systems integration has been an elusive goal for planners and policy makers, and until recently there has been little empirical evidence that integration, when achieved, leads to better client outcomes.[7] Roland Warren and his colleagues found that 1960s

Model Cities programs, designed to increase coordination and innovation among urban social service agencies, accomplished neither innovation nor coordination because gatekeeping organizations defined a narrow range of objectives for social reform and resisted change.[8] Coordination is often done around trivial matters by organizations that systematically exclude those with controversial agendas.[9] Moreover, attempts at comprehensive planning and service integration disregard the fact that many issues, such as federal economic policy and its effect on unemployment, are beyond the scope of local or regional efforts.[10] Finally, Warren argues, defining the solution to poverty in terms of social service strategies leaves the causes of poverty and attendant social problems unexamined and shifts attention to clients' personal deficiencies.[11]

For outreach workers, bureaucratic impediments are a matter not of theory but of the day-to-day texture of the work. Even before outreach projects for homeless mentally ill persons can be put in place, there must be a decision to serve this group when other clients who are seen as "motivated" for treatment are already taxing the resources of public mental health agencies. When funding opportunities or public pressure pushes agencies to accept this new clientele, doubts about the new mission will wax when outreach workers refer clients for continuing care and thus add to the caseloads of overburdened clinicians.[12] Outreach workers also face attitudes and practices that are antithetical to effective work on the street. Traditional mental health practice tends to screen out the nonclinical content of the individual's homeless life and circumscribe problems according to clinical solutions that the discipline has to offer. Outreach workers struggle to build on the homeless person's strengths, but they may do so within institutions that historically have seen clients as problems to be contained rather than as individuals with uncharted possibilities.

Social factors are an integral part of the institutional context of outreach work, but the direction of influence is not clear-cut. Do categorical distinctions for allocating resources to the poor originate in institutional power to shape public attitudes, or do these institutions merely follow the dictates of the public will? Most likely the influence flows both ways. For this report, though, the center of a web of influence within which the homeless encounter takes place is the social service network of which the outreach program is a part.

THE INSTITUTIONAL CONTEXT OF BOUNDARY ENCOUNTERS

For everything about boundary encounters that identifies them as new and different, there are countervailing institutional elements that predate them, shape them, and mark off the field in which they take place. Going out of doors, outreach workers take with them an internal office consisting of program and funding guidelines, social norms, and professional training. These elements affect their moment-to-moment encounters with homeless persons and the offer of services and citizenship they can make. Wearing an innovator's hat, the outreach worker pushes bureaucracy out into the community. Wearing an official's hat, the same worker directs street-level encounters into traditional channels. If homeless persons have control over the time and location of their initial meetings with workers, then workers chip away at this control by scheduling meetings in settings more official than highway bridges or abandoned vehicles behind the Jiffy Lube. If workers offer choices from a wide range of services, then funding agencies and host organizations define certain services as paramount. These essential services drive the work, and homeless persons must be persuaded to accept them.

Service organizations, as Michael Lipsky has convincingly demonstrated, embody contradictory impulses to alleviate suffering while controlling and limiting requests from those who are suffering.[13] To manage these contradictions and a high volume of work, policy makers and social service organizations designate subgroups of the poor along lines of disciplinary expertise. Mental illness, substance abuse, and homelessness, much as they are concrete social problems, are also bureaucratic categories. Categorization may also be motivated by distinctions between putatively deserving and undeserving persons. Means tests for the instrumental relief of suffering effectively define those who do not pass the test as having neither the external stigmata of suffering (since they have not qualified for relief from them) nor the internal experience of suffering (since they brought it upon themselves).

Categorical requirements are given to workers who seek out clients. Outreach workers who observe people eating at soup kitchens are usually correct in assuming they are poor, but when they determine that these individuals are not homeless, they can move on in the search for their target population. Even within the homeless population, further distinctions such as mental illness, substance abuse, or HIV infection are used to distribute services. If workers, understandably, feel guilty about turning away those who do not meet program criteria, they will have a strong incentive to decide that those who do qualify are especially deserving of the services they get. Program clients can further earn the label of "deserving" by appreciating staff efforts and responding to interventions in ways that the funding agency or the program itself has defined in advance as signs of improvement. These signs may be measured over short periods of time, as dictated, in part, by the need to gather outcome data on a large number of clients. Thus the question of what happens to people over the long haul may remain unanswered.

A physician assistant with a homeless health care project in New Haven talked about her frustration with categorical funding. Her reference points may be dated and local, but her general point is relevant today:

> I come from a training of family practice where you try to embrace as wide a unit as possible. Categorical grants run contrary to that. A lot of energy goes into trying to sort people out, and I'm not sure it's worth it. Once someone has started drinking, you can't get them into the mental health system. The door is shut. I had a patient who figured that out. He had a psychiatric

history and he was into drugs. To get into the mental health system he put a gun to his mouth, called the police, and said, "I'm about to shoot myself." He got in. He planned it.

The New Haven ACCESS project's criteria included homeless persons who were dually diagnosed with mental illness and substance abuse. They excluded those with "primary" substance abuse and those whose mental illness was "secondary" to their use of drugs. But distinctions between primary and secondary forms of mental illness may reveal as much about bureaucratic and professional turf-staking as about scientific consensus. Even when scientific consensus has been reached and research instruments have been tested in the field, human beings must make judgment calls about eligibility in some cases. Different workers and evaluators with the New Haven project might have accepted or rejected the man who put the gun to his head, based on idiosyncrasies of interpretation and attitude and a glut or dearth of referrals needed to meet program quotas. In addition, different programs will have different interpretations of homelessness and mental illness. In New Haven, the ACCESS project had federal program criteria that favored longtime homeless street people with untreated mental illnesses. Clinicians from the host mental health center, however, favored longtime patients who were "houseless" (doubled up with family or staying temporarily with friends) but not literally homeless. Unofficial interpretations such as the latter, and the requests that flow from them, put pressure on outreach teams. Outreach workers may respond by cutting tacit deals with inpatient clinicians to relax criteria in order to secure a hospital bed for a homeless individual at a later time.

Categorical funding may fuel divisions on the street, encouraging self-fulfilling prophecies about the unworthiness of those who do not qualify for services. Mental health outreach workers are given constant reminders of willful disobedience in the behavior of substance abusers. This can lead to a street-level contempt of those whom workers are bound by contract to reject. It is hard not to feel that the addict who badgers you for housing needs it less than the mentally ill person who has to be coaxed into accepting a cup of coffee. Even those who believe that addiction is a disease and not a form of criminal behavior run across enough sociopathic addicts to soften the hard edge of their guilt over denying services to substance abusers. A formerly homeless person, at the vantage point of recovery from addiction, had this to say as a staff member about addicts:

> The substance abuse person, they feel that they're getting over: "This is something I'm getting for nothing." Whereas the hard-luck story is very appreciative. It shows, the way they carry themselves. Even in the line at a soup kitchen when they're being provided food. Say it's something they don't care to eat. [The hard luck person is] still appreciative. The substance abuse person? "Franks and beans again, franks and beans again . . ."

Yet homeless addicts' anger often came in response to rejection. Had they been members of the target population—which, in New Haven, they had been a few years earlier—it is likely that their behavior with workers would have changed dramatically. In other conversations with me, the worker who spoke just above reflected the ambivalence we feel toward those whom we must reject, criticizing the ingratitude of substance abusers at one time and defending their need for treatment at another.

The advantage of categorical services is that they bring a specific expertise to bear on individuals with specific problems. And to point out the inequities of categorical funding is not to conclude that generic funding is the obvious solution. Such an approach would bring with it the problem of providing comprehensive services to a much larger group and would shift the categorical focus from the homeless person's disability to homelessness itself. Battles over conflicting definitions of homelessness, written by funding agencies or service providers that are bound to represent their own and their clients' interests, might then be waged as fiercely as when other categorical hairs were available for splitting.

The stigmata of symptoms and diagnoses are not merely individual signs of distress, but categories for moving people through social service programs. "The processing of people into clients, assigning them to categories for treatment by bureaucrats, and treating them in terms of those categories, is a social process," Lipsky writes. "Client characteristics do not exist outside of the process that gives rise to them."[14] Clients, like workers, he contends, are caught in conflicting roles. They are citizens who might be expected to lobby for their rights, and "bureaucratic subjects" who learn to adjust their demands to the resources and habits of their service providers. At an individual level, people-processing teaches clients to regard themselves as categorical entities rather than individuals. At the collective level, it isolates clients and inhibits their concerted action.[15]

And there is the problem of quotas. In New Haven, the pressure to meet required enrollment in the national outcome study tempted workers to relax their criteria or select those who were less severely mentally ill than others but easier to enroll. On the street, ineligible homeless persons were aware of the numbers game and, in the early stages of the project, found ways to fake symptoms in order to be admitted to the program. Having accepted these individuals when numbers were down, workers could feel hoodwinked when these same individuals showed their true colors and be tempted to discharge them, especially if numbers had gone up and the pressure to enroll had eased. Workers, asked to manage these conflicting demands, might be forgiven if they were to look at some homeless persons during good census times and ask themselves, "Do I have time for this? Can't somebody else refer him for substance abuse treatment? He won't go anyway."

Workers found ways to assuage their moral qualms about excluding those who did not meet their criteria:

> I went to [a shelter] and there was a client that we had engaged in the past. It's obvious that he doesn't meet our criteria. He needs housing, of course. He approached me and said, "What's happening, what's going on?" I said, "Tony, you don't meet our criteria. I can make some housing referrals for you." He said, "You mean to tell me I have to be crazy in order to get help? I

need help." I said, "I'm not saying you have to be crazy in order to get help. These are the criteria, and there are other programs. I can make a referral." He was upset. I didn't really feel bad because I can't cure the world. It's not that I didn't have compassion for him, but I know my power is limited. I was able to distance myself.

Some researchers have noted that when problems of marginal persons are seen as being primarily pathological rather than social in nature, the medical profession becomes the major source of expertise and the social aspects of the problem are masked.[16] Political decisions that both precede and sustain the medical solution are also obscured. In a service environment that focuses on long-term mental illness among homeless people, less chronic forms of mental illness may be neglected.[17] The notion that homelessness itself may be a "crazy-making" condition[18] is given a polite nod but has little impact on policies and programs. In addition, medical classifications with built-in middle-class biases may distort our perceptions of disability or disobedience among homeless persons. A mentally stable individual who acts according to the behavioral demands of street life may fit the diagnostic criteria for having antisocial personality disorder,[19] and thus may or may not meet the criteria for a given categorical program. Mental health outreach workers in New Haven never lost sight of the social and economic causes of homelessness, but their response was channeled through clinical structures. For hard-pressed workers, discussions about the appropriateness of given criteria can seem moot—the categorical lines have been drawn and workers are now caring for seriously ill individuals—until other programs come along and reject their clients on different categorical grounds.

The context of social problems and efforts to address them may qualify the negative aspects of categorical services. The mental health profession, much as it may limit one's view of unique individuals, also defends individual care. In New Haven, outreach workers' advocacy for better treatment of mentally ill persons in one particular shelter appeared to benefit all homeless persons who stayed there. In this case, mental health expertise and clinical-ethical standards effected a gradual shift in shelter business as usual. But the same contextual caveat may apply in reverse. Howard Goldman and Joseph Morrissey have cogently argued that the current, "fourth cycle" of mental health reform is qualitatively different from previous institutional reform efforts, which defined social problems as mental health problems. In the current cycle, the problems of poor, chronically mentally ill persons are seen as social welfare problems requiring a wide range of treatment, housing, and rehabilitation services.[20] Yet if homeless outreach teams provide a model for socially enlightened mental health care, crisscrossing currents and tensions, such as the relative weight given to clinical stability or to housing, the relative status of clinicians and rehabilitation providers, and the subtleties of integrating clinical care and social needs, continue to exert their influences.

In New Haven, there was a dynamic tension behind the alternating use of the terms *patient* and *client*. Clinical leaders generally favored the former; case managers and rehabilitation specialists favored the latter. A national evaluator visiting the project noted that the New Haven project was one of the few ACCESS sites that used the term *patient* at all. Over time, as the project became established as a clinical undertaking within the host mental health center, *patient* became the normative, though not exclusive, term. It may be that the New Haven project adhered more closely than other ACCESS projects to traditional clinical practice. More likely, though, it was adapting to its local, traditional circumstances. As a new program within a mental health system that was wary of taking on responsibility for New Haven's social problems, the project had to build respect for its clinical operation. This is not to say that it settled for clinical business as usual, but that its location on a spectrum from clinical to social welfare approaches was influenced by its professional and institutional environment.

For Lipsky, publicly funded human service organizations are both gatekeepers and advocates. They espouse the ideal of individual care but maintain bureaucratic distance.[21] At the street level, workers are given the impossible task of resolving society's ambivalence toward the poor.[22] "Social workers have a caring function, but they also have a punitive function," said the physician assistant who spoke earlier. "If you get identified too much with institutional practices, it cuts you off." For this worker, her professional code of practice was a counterweight to bureaucratic requirements to process people swiftly through the medical system:

> As a medical provider, by law we have a lot of latitude. I have a code of practice that I'm able to insist upon as long as it's standard care. I'm supposed to see x number of patients every afternoon, but if a patient had a cold and when I examine their mouth they have oral thrush, they now have a potentially catastrophic diagnosis. That's more than a fifteen-minute visit. It's going to take a lot more medical involvement, which might mean institutional things get botched up in a clinic. My license gives me the latitude to say, "That's just the way that's got to be."

With increased attention to the costs of contemporary health care, one wonders whether this individual's code of practice will continue to give her such latitude.

Street-level work forces the worker to look beyond categorical or clinical perspectives to see the social environment in which people struggle. But bureaucratic demands assert themselves in outreach work as well. There is endless paperwork designed to meet good standards of clinical care. There may be research forms to be filled out. And there are the criteria for traditional programs to which outreach workers will eventually refer their clients. Such criteria may require molding clients, on paper or in person, to get them the services they need.[23]

Lipsky points out that street-level efforts to improve individual client care are almost preordained to fail because they are organizationally counterproductive. Increasing the ability to serve clients will lead to increased demand for services. Assuming no increase in resources, this will eventually lead to a rationing of services.[24] The introduction of managed care and competition for contracts to serve the poor, with corresponding demands for efficiency and increased client contact, may alter this equation. Or it may change only the location of tension points. Workers may find themselves seeing more clients and using ever more sophisticated information-management systems to reduce time spent on paperwork, but their increased efficiency may not benefit their clients. If workers have less time and less discretion to make services conform to individual client needs, then those who need the services most may be least able to get them.

Bureaucratic and social processes locate problems in the individual while mass-producing programmatic responses. In Lipsky's organizational world, street-level bureaucrats manage irreconcilable client and organizational demands by scaling back on their hopes for clients. At the same time, they find ways to rationalize their participation in tainted service delivery by maintaining allegiance to the ideal of individual care. The institution, too, pays lip service to "putting the client first" without disturbing the mechanisms for producing impersonal units of service.[25] At the edge of society, the worker's desire to provide services can veer off into the advocate's desire to redistribute the wealth. But organizations, which carefully parcel out resources in order to ensure their survival, hold advocacy in check.

The process of separation and reduced hope flows up and down the organizational ladder as workers confront their inability to solve the social and economic problems of homeless persons.[26] In mental health outreach work, Linda Chafetz writes, clients and workers sometimes make mutual unspoken decisions to lower their expectations. For workers, those decisions may be based on a lack of resources to support the progress of homeless persons over the long run, or a lack of belief that such progress is even possible for their more seriously mentally ill clients. They may also be based on a retreat to biological or clinical explanations and techniques that fail to take into account the social and economic environment of homeless persons.[27]

Workers may resort to "creaming"—selecting for help those individuals who are most likely to succeed or least difficult to manage. The practice of creaming helps workers to meet quotas and may leave more room for intensive efforts with a few, more seriously disturbed individuals who require more staff time and energy. In adopting such strategies, workers are not placing their mission in jeopardy so much as redefining it out of jeopardy.

Mental health outreach workers face homeless persons who have disabilities that preceded their homelessness and further scars from their daily battles for survival. Workers also make their way through a tangled web of bureaucratic and traditional service approaches in order to be effective on the street. And they move homeless people into housing with no assurance that their long-term prospects are much better than their current situations.

There is hope for double-bound workers and their homeless clients, though. Lipsky, while documenting the dilemmas of public workers, also points out the power they possess to distribute resources. Street-level bureaucrats operate under the guidelines of public policy and institutional procedures, but effectively create their own policy through day-to-day decisions, routines, and adjustments to uncertainty.[28] The wide area of discretion they exercise can be used for adjusting to mediocrity or for breaking down institutional barriers. If outreach workers devise street-level policies that correspond to their reduced hopes in the face of insoluble poverty, they also devise policies that can erode institutional immobility. It appears that workers are moved toward the latter efforts by their encounters with devastation. The *moral* imperative, perhaps piqued by guilt, that comes with street work is channeled through a *clinical* imperative (which

I shall return to in the last section of this chapter) to embrace personal responsibility for the client.[29] Such a conceptual model helps workers to maintain the passion they require for their work. But even this is not enough.

THE SOCIAL PSYCHOLOGY OF THE HOMELESS OUTREACH TEAM

Outreach workers do not manage their dilemmas alone. They go out in pairs in search of homeless people. They provide services in collaboration with other clinicians, case managers, and rehabilitation specialists. Around and above these shifting groups, there is the project team as a whole. The team has the practical function of organizing and managing the work. It is a caring community, even a substitute or transitional family, for homeless people. It is a family, if sometimes a troubled one, for workers, a place of refuge for airing frustrations and exulting in victories. The team is the place where the ethos of the work is defined, defended, and modified over time. And the team is the place where the dilemmas and contradictions of outreach work are addressed by the project as a whole. The need to manage these contradictions increases in proportion to the tension between individual care and organizational needs and the resulting constraints on workers. The team, then, can support workers to individually and collectively resist bureaucratization and continue to place a high value on serving unique individuals.[30]

In this, the most speculative section of my report, I speak in general terms, extrapolating from my experience with one outreach project, but I do not claim to speak for all homeless outreach teams. I offer this analysis because I think the team or group effort is an essential ingredient in what makes work at the margins feasible over the long term, and because I think we need to gain a better understanding of how the team helps outreach workers maintain their stamina and ideals on the streets. Some of the themes in this section, such as scapegoating, idealization of the group, and achievement of solidarity through finding a common enemy or opponent, are, of course, familiar elements in group psychology, but I speak of their particular applications to outreach teams.

I identify six archetypal players that contribute to the team's status and help it to define and support the work. They are the essential or mythical client, the essential or mythical worker, the scapegoat, the rebel, the leader, and the team as a collective player. My archetypal players do not fit neatly with specific individuals on the project I studied, nor will they fit neatly with those on other projects. An individual worker or supervisor may play more than one of the four archetypal staff roles—essential worker, scapegoat, rebel, and leader—and any one archetypal staff role may be played by more than one worker. (All workers have a touch of the rebel in them.) Some archetypal figures may be present as latent tendencies and emerge only during crises. Even the meaning of *team* will differ according to the idiosyncrasies of its members, the plans and accidents of the project's founding, and other local conditions.

THE ESSENTIAL CLIENT

The essential client personifies the hopes that outreach workers have for homeless persons. Her story is both harrowing and touching, and she will attract an enormous investment of staff time and energy. She is often—though not in the case of Peggy, whose story follows—linked ineluctably with one worker. She may, like Peggy, be a success by almost any objective measure, or her success may be more limited, remarkable only by contrast with her status when outreach workers met her.

Peggy, a fifty-two-year-old African American female, had suffered from mental illness for years but had dropped out of treatment. Outreach workers found her at her home on the West Haven Green. (West Haven is a town contiguous to New Haven.) She dressed in many layers of purple clothes. Workers surmised that purple was her color of mourning. She wore five rings on each finger and twenty chains around her neck. She waved around a plastic Luke Skywalker sword when strangers came near her. Peggy was a patron saint to homeless people on the West Haven Green, requiring outreach workers to bring clothes and food for her friends as the price of conversation with her.

After bringing her cigarettes, coffee, and purple clothes for a few months, workers began to piece together her story. Peggy had endured many tragedies. Two of her children died in a house fire. One of her sisters was killed in a freak accident and another was dying of cancer. Peggy refused the services that workers offered because the project received federal funds and she thought the government wanted to imprison her for her past work with Amnesty International. Her rejection of help was also connected to her anger toward family members who were trying to get her into mental health treatment, thus demonstrating to her their unwillingness to deal with her tragedy. Perhaps Peggy also saw mental health treatment as forcing her to talk about the losses in her life. She was not prepared to do that.

One day Peggy agreed to visit Columbus House to take a shower. Later, she washed her clothes there and even took a peek at the sleeping quarters, but declined to spend the night. A few weeks later, the West Haven police brought her to an emergency room after she threatened them for removing the clothes with which she had dressed a statue of a Civil War hero. Peggy told outreach workers that she did not see them as being associated with the inpatient unit where she was committed (although they were), but as outsiders who could get her released. She signed up with the outreach project, was discharged to Columbus House shelter, and promptly tossed out the psychiatric medications she had had to take while in the hospital. She was furious when her aunt gained legal conservatorship of her, but her anger drew her closer to her workers. Her sister died, and two workers accompanied her to the funeral. She found an apartment, renewed her beautician's license, and was planning to get back to work.

Workers traded anecdotes about their recent encounters with Peggy, comparing her to the wild woman in purple who waved around her Luke Skywalker sword on the West Haven Green. She became a marker point around which the team built morale against high caseloads, mountains of clinical paperwork, and wild-eyed managers waving around figures on low research-enrollment figures and follow-up rates. Workers were wary of Peggy's progress, though, because she refused to acknowledge that she had a mental illness. They feared that although she was doing well now, it might be only a matter of time before she had another breakdown. They hoped to keep a strong connection with Peggy and help her to avoid becoming homeless again.[31]

There are several elements to Peggy's mythical status. She had been a "treatment failure" in more traditional programs. She forced outreach workers to draw on every professional and emotional resource they could muster. After pushing them to their limits by rejecting their help, she relented, got better, and was grateful to workers who reached out to her. Furthermore, her severe disability seemed to guarantee that she would continue to need the team's support for some time. And finally, while workers have a hard time letting go of their favorite clients, stories such as Peggy's give them hope that their clients can reach the stage of moving beyond the need for outreach workers and their services.

Peggy achieved mythical status in spite of not matching the essential client profile in two respects. First, essential clients appear most often during the early, formative phase of the outreach project, when much critical staff learning is done. Peggy was not enrolled until the New Haven project had entered its third year and its basic outlines were firmly in place. Second, most essential clients are paired with an essential worker who gains his status through a baptism by fire with that homeless individual. In Peggy's case, several workers did important work with her and none stood out over the others. Perhaps the project had matured to the point where it needed fewer essential clients and could pair those it found with the team as a whole. It remains to be seen, though, whether Peggy, as a latecomer and lacking a staff partner, will be able to maintain her mythical stature over time.

THE ESSENTIAL WORKER

If the essential client can ride into the outreach team's consciousness on the strength of her own charisma, the essential worker cannot. Any outreach worker worth his salt has the tools and the innate capacity to achieve mythical stature, but only those who have been paired with an essential client can become essential themselves.

Jack is white and in his mid-forties. He had been a longtime paraprofessional worker in a state institution, and might have stayed on to become a state "lifer" waiting out his time until pension but for a car accident that caused him to leave his job. Later, with a freeze on state hiring in effect, he joined the outreach team. Andrea, his homeless partner, is African American and in her early forties. She had five children by her alcoholic husband. Her husband left her, and she lost custody of her children because her organic brain deficits made it impossible for her to care for them. Jack first met Andrea in a corner of an abandoned parking garage in New Haven, where she lived with her alcoholic boyfriend, who was found dead one morning. Andrea was fond of telling anyone who would listen that "Jack never treated me like trash."

The central event of Jack and Andrea's relationship (briefly mentioned in the last chapter) occurred on the coldest day of a very cold year. The team feared that Andrea would die on the streets that night. Jack and another worker had found an apartment for her, but she refused to take it. It appeared that for Andrea, accepting housing in New Haven meant the end of her dream of moving to Georgia to be with her children again. Jack pleaded with her for hours, pointing out that many people had summer homes in the North and winter homes in the South and that Andrea might one day have the same. Finally, risking his carefully cultivated relationship with her, he feigned disgust and walked away. Andrea immediately agreed to take the apartment. With rocky moments, she has been housed ever since.

Sandy, an early-thirties white social worker, had worked mostly on inpatient medical units before joining the outreach team. Her trial by fire was Monk, a white veteran who had lived on the streets for twenty years. When he first met Sandy, Monk was troubled by visions or memories of having worked with a terrorist group during the early 1970s on a plot to overthrow Saigon. His anger—against Newt Gingrich and the Republican right, against all those who had "provoked" him to fights in forty-seven states in the union—was frightening to behold. Even the local homeless advocacy group had grown weary of his relentless song of social oppression.

Monk's delusions and his behavior seemed to be connected to a childhood of violence and abuse. Sandy was able to withstand his anger at her for representing both the "phony" clinicians who had tried to control his life and his sister who had rejected him. Although she helped Monk find an apartment and persuaded him to accept mental health treatment, the defining moment of their relationship occurred when Monk sat in Sandy's office one day and called his sister in California. This call led to a family reunion and reconciliation.

Ed is African American, in his early thirties, and was homeless for a time before joining the team as an outreach worker. He had no previous human service experience, but his street savvy and natural skills combined to give him an edge in persuading the most alienated individuals to accept help. His homeless partner is Daniel, who, as noted earlier, spent his childhood in foster homes, and who suffered from the disabilities of severe mental illness, substance abuse, HIV infection, and end-stage failure of two vital organs.

Ed got to know Daniel through serving food with him at a New Haven soup kitchen where Daniel volunteered. The defining moment of their relationship took place when Ed tried to coax Daniel into treatment for his cocaine use in exchange for placing him in a subsidized apartment. "No!" Daniel shouted. "In 1978 they took the alcohol away from me! In 1982 they took the marijuana away from me! In 1989 they took the heroin away from me! And now you want to take the cocaine away from me and you're not going do it! I'll cut back, I'll use twice a month, but I'm not going to stop!" Ed hesitated, reviewing everything he had learned about using housing as leverage for treatment. "All right," he said. Daniel took the apartment and has kept it, with a moderate cocaine habit and frequent trips to the hospital because of his deteriorating physical condition. He continues to see Ed and visits a social club for psychiatric patients.

Each of these workers made a lasting connection with an individual who had been cut off from all social service programs and most human contact. Jack earned his essential stature through faithfulness to his self-espoused principle of "unconditional positive regard" and by taking a risk that paid off on the coldest day of the year. Sandy navigated the dangerous shoals of Monk's attraction-revulsion for her and helped him reconnect to a family that, to his surprise, wanted him back. For Ed, the way in was his dogged persistence and the risk he took in breaking a rule of treatment in order to get Daniel off the streets.

THE SCAPEGOAT

The scapegoat is rarely incompetent. More often, he accepts the ethos of the work but lacks personal comfort in the field. Or he is unwilling to help others with their clients and cannot share his own. Or his personal and work lives are too rigidly separated, or not separated enough. He may be socially awkward and difficult to talk to. If he is an outreach worker, he inhibits the flow and volume of the work. If he is a supervisor, he may fail to support his staff. But the scapegoat provides symbolic benefits to the team that partly compensate for his practical deficits. First, by being a nominal team member but failing to act like one, he does what office-based workers and hidebound institutions cannot do: he proves that experience alone does not make an outreach worker. Time on the streets is essential, of course. The work will sharpen or awaken inner qualities for the chosen few, but it cannot implant these qualities in a barren heart. The outreach worker must have the right stuff to begin with. Second, as the staff person who seems to symbolize both "undeserving" homeless persons and unhelpful institutions, the scapegoat allows team members to act out their antipathies toward recalcitrant homeless persons and institutions within the safety of the team. Third, the scapegoat, by taking on the role of "he who does not get it," helps team members to avoid facing the degree to which they don't get it, either—don't really feel comfortable in the field, suspect they lack the social imagination to cross the border into the homeless person's world, or worst of all, fear that "getting it" is not enough because their interventions are powerless against the behemoth of urban poverty.

As should be clear from these comments, I am not arguing that the scapegoat is blameless, only that he becomes a lightning rod for feelings and frustrations that include, but go beyond, whatever deficiencies he may have.

THE REBEL

The rebel is an individualist and a born enemy of bureaucracy. If part of the scapegoat's function is to represent symbolically the negative side of workers' ambivalence toward homeless persons—all that is frustrating and reprehensible in them—then the rebel symbolizes all that is romantic and free about homeless persons. Personally, the rebel is independent but not a loner, a team member but an aristocrat.

On the street, the rebel stance reduces cultural barriers. The armor of rebel replaces the armor of strict professional, becoming a kind of substitute class and lending the appearance of near equality with people who are homeless. The rebel stance involves more than casual clothes. It is a style and attitude that shows respect for homeless individuals and comfort with contingency.

Within the team, the rebel is part hero, part court jester. She shows how far scorn for administrative entanglements can go without becoming insubordination. She reminds the leader of his dual roles as bureaucrat who protects the team from bureaucracy and secret rebel who will never sell out the team to institutional mediocrity. By testing where the leader stands, the rebel helps to locate the team on a scale that has the street at one end and the institution at the other. By paying him the backhanded compliment of admiring his political skill, she voices the team's understanding that the leader must absorb an institutional taint in order to reduce the taint that shadows outreach workers on the streets.

Within the institution, the rebel's stance helps her to keep bureaucracy at a psychological arm's length. It sets a tone for the institution to temper its demands on the project during its early development, treating the project as a mischievous stepchild— in the organization but not of it. The rebel meets agency requirements but maintains her dignity; the organization stops short of demanding total obeisance. The rebel must live with the anxiety of being the person who pushes the edge of the organizational envelope, and with the possibility that her compatriots will abandon her if she goes too far. She prevails, though, because of her competence as a worker, winning respect from her team and the host organization.

The rebel's stance is that of the maverick rather than the organizer who directly challenges social service systems. In one sense, this stance is a distorted reflection of an individual, pathologizing approach to social problems. In another, it enables the rebel to establish partnerships with homeless rebels at the margins. But there is danger in the margins. The rebel risks rending the veil of an illusion that she herself helps to maintain. Her mocking questions of recalcitrant institutions and office-based workers may come back to mock her, whispering in her ear that programs alone cannot turn many lives around, and rebels alone cannot change powerful institutions.

The Leader

The leader must spend time on the streets if he is to have credibility on the team. He must be able to reflect, espouse, and help create the essential lessons and values of the project. He must be part of and yet apart from the team, and he must teach by example how the irreconcilable demands of the work can be provisionally reconciled at the organizational level.

The leader acts as a buffer, protecting the team from overweening institutional scrutiny in the early stages so that it can implement boundary-breaking techniques and gain credibility in the homeless community. He agrees to wear more of the stigmata of bureaucracy than the worker is allowed to exhibit on the street. He good-naturedly bears the rebel's insults, showing the team that he can wear his taint with dignity and thus that they perhaps can wear their lesser taint. Within the host organization or social service system, he demonstrates that one can be wise as a serpent, not merely outraged over institutional barriers. At the same time, he must demonstrate that the team's outrage on behalf of its clients will stimulate him to push for organizational change.

The leader guides the team through the early days of creative "effervescence,"[32] as staff rally around the urgency of their clients' needs and the conviction that they can cut through all barriers which slow their rescue operation. But high energy and communal passion for the work must recede. At this time, the leader's chief function is to guide the team into an organizational phase of development while helping it to maintain a sense of its original purity. He must encode the innovative elements of the work while putting in place a structure that can survive over time. On the practical level, he attempts to transform informal practice into policy. On the expressive level, he, with others, attempts to institutionalize charisma. Program successes such as housing the reluctant Andrea when she was in danger of freezing on the streets can be enshrined as myths that teach the program's ethic. Nonbureaucratic principles such as "Do not take no for an answer" can be used to create a different kind of bureaucracy. Such tactics help outreach workers to retain the badge of outsiders while continuing to work within the larger social service system.[33]

The Team as a Collective Player

As the organizational unit for managing the work, the team must be flexible enough to adjust to the day-to-day contingency of street-level work and to shifts in local economic and social conditions. The team is also a culture-making entity, the focal point for transforming individual workers' perceptions and yearnings into collective values and practices. It is the repository of group wisdom, the place where cynicism and routine are managed and social imagination is nurtured, even after the secret or specialness of the work has partly fallen to the group's own technical knowledge of itself. The team represents the essence of the work and stands in relationship to all that is not-team. At one end, not-team is the homeless community itself. The team establishes the moral imperative of its clinical and rehabilitative mission to compensate for the uneasy line of separation that workers have drawn between themselves and their clients. At the other end, not-team is all staff and institutions that impede the team's work and fail to share its values.

As other archetypal players lose their magic, the team picks up the slack. Essential clients continue to inspire, but they may not retain the charisma they had during the project's infancy. The clinical work that contributed to their success is better understood and can, to some degree, be reproduced with other clients. As workers' knowledge increases, they become ever so little more the technicians. The scapegoat no longer arouses fierce passions, only a shrug and a sigh. The rebel grows weary. She has gone to the wall too many times to continue to lead the charge. The leader maintains his managerial function, but if he has done his job of institutionalizing charisma, his visionary function is no longer critical. If he has not done his job, then he has lost his own magic because of this failure. The team consoles its individual members for their gradual loss of personal charisma by substituting the magic of the team as a collective visionary entity moving through time and bureaucratic warfare.

In the early stages of the project, the team builds group cohesion and honors workers who have a low status within their own service systems. Later, the team helps workers adjust to their status as veterans and elder statesmen, now more accepted by their peers, who are working with homeless clients whom those workers referred to them. New programs built on the project's work may prove to be an invigorating point-counterpoint for the team. Outreach workers, if respected for their wisdom, can become teachers and cultural icons. If workers are resented for the same qualities, the team has a new competitor, even enemy, against which to hone its sense of uniqueness. The team may remember its uniqueness, almost lost to itself, as it sees that newcomers, regardless of their zeal and commitment, will never be able to capture the freshness of the team's first forays into the alien culture of homelessness.

There is a risk, in discussing archetypal players, of giving the reader a static, hermetic view of outreach work. The team and its players evolve over time. Outside forces—a loss or gain of local resources, the impending end of funding, staff turnover, and other factors—impinge on the program. The old days were never that new and the new days are never that old. When workers look back, they are not simply reminiscing, but performing what Bennett Berger calls the "ideological work" of balancing their values with the contingencies and external constraints that chip away at those values. Circumstances give practical worth to values and beliefs, but also reveal the ambiguities of values and beliefs. The effort to routinize ideals, the raw material from which visionary projects are constructed, may result in modifying or abandoning them. Ideological work is self-serving, but never only self-serving. It involves holding up values in one hand and self-serving interests or external demands in the other, and seeing how or whether they can coexist without forcing participants to either sell out their beliefs or die out from their refusal to adapt beliefs to circumstances.[34]

In New Haven, an ideological framework was given to the outreach project by previous research and by grant guidelines, but the team needed to fill out this framework with its own idealistic nuances and in relation to local conditions. Workers found various aids. One was a clinical-humanistic orientation that contrasted with the regimentation and judgmental actions of emergency shelter staff. Another was the sense of being a rescue operation in the midst of social disaster that could become physical disaster. "People could die" became a rallying cry for interventions on the street during the winter months. These aids helped the team to stake out its uniqueness even while categorizing those who would receive help. Ideological work involved managing the real and apparent conflicts between the relative importance of clinical and rehabilitative work, the client's homelessness and the client's mental illness, and client choice and the clinician's skills in persuading the client to accept mental health treatment.

There is nothing new about the team concept, nor is teamwork an innate good. Its underside is a potential loss of focus and personal responsibility among team members, and it may be ill adapted in some settings. The team, like its archetypal players, does not exist in pure form. It is a concept as well as a program unit, and it is always in flux, shaping itself through a dynamic working out of its own dilemmas. When successful, it enables workers to maintain the flexibility they need in their work and a sense of solidarity with homeless persons.

PROGRAM CITIZENSHIP

The ultimate question about outreach workers and outreach teams is whether they can make a difference in many homeless persons' lives. A program can be successful as programs go but a failure in larger social terms. Or it may be successful in creating clients who gain the benefits of clienthood but are unable to achieve a positive identity in society. In the early 1980s, Ellen Baxter and Kim Hopper cautioned against a tendency to regard human service programs as the answer to the crisis of homelessness in America:

> A service perspective which sees problems as ultimately amenable to the ministrations of skilled "providers," if only the right mix of services and mode of delivery can be devised, is a deluded one. The reason is simple: the problems of the homeless run deeper than the services which mental health and social service professionals can supply.[35]

Fifteen years later, with an increasing reliance on these professionals, we may ask whether Baxter and Hopper's original point is now moot. Homelessness, after all, can be a resource opportunity. Certain housing options are available only to homeless persons with disabilities such as mental illness, substance abuse, or HIV infection. Health care projects for the homeless may provide more comprehensive care than other health care programs for the poor. Emergency shelters are expanding to offer transitional housing. Social service programs that have sprung up around homelessness may provide a substitute niche for surplus people who cannot find a place within mainstream society.[36] Those who use these programs well may find they can be a ticket to first-class citizenship. Others may find they provide another poverty niche, with substandard housing and social isolation in place of emergency shelters and homeless companions in misery, a ticket to second-class or "program" citizenship in place of the shadow citizenship of homelessness. Program citizenship may substitute for a loss of work and social and family relationships, but it may also discourage people from reconnecting with family and friends and their own lost skills. Eventually, as Jacqueline Wiseman observes, public institutions can become the only source of mainstream social contact in the lives of many marginal persons.[37]

Different streams of influence—bequeathed values and techniques, the experience of street work, and the personal characteristics of homeless persons and outreach workers—come together to shape how clients, workers, and the nature of the work are seen. This process, which might be called shadow ideological work, parallels the conscious ideological work of defining values. Outreach workers use motivation, symptomatology, diagnoses, and other tools to guide them in this work. These become the points with which they build an argument about homeless individuals in order to sell them as worthy clients. There is a risk, though, that over time, the argument they have fashioned for others may become the image they see as well.

While boundary encounters are located within a nexus of institutional constraints and social problems that come close to negating them, they still represent a break with traditional practice. This break seems to be a function of at least four factors. One is the location of boundary transactions at the edge of institutional influence and scrutiny. A second is the survival experiences of individuals who can hardly be expected to step straight into traditional client roles. The third is that the conditions of homeless life defeat traditional modes of social and clinical practice. The fourth is that the encounter with the person within his environment, while it can wear workers down with a sense of futility, also keeps them alive in their work.

Eventually, though, workers' focus must shift from the streets to the community that will house their clients and to the agencies that will provide social services to them. Homeless persons, including those with mental illnesses, want what most of us want—normal housing in good areas, with autonomy, privacy, and safety.[38] Mentally ill homeless persons want help in obtaining resources, but often do not want staff supervising their movements.[39] Having a home involves expressive as well as instrumental needs, a sense of control over one's life and the ability to create one's own environment. It involves creating or reclaiming one's personal identity as a housed person with social and community status and respect.[40]

The needs of homeless people are deep and wide. Outreach workers feel a special urgency to break down boundaries that slow their efforts. But even when workers can deliver the basic goods of housing, medical treatment, and income supports, the long-term prospects for homeless persons who accept their offers are uncertain. Workers cannot give their clients a social support network or new work skills and job prospects, nor can they solve the social problems that engendered the current brand of homelessness in America and threaten to make it a permanent fixture on our social landscape.

In the end, it may be the unfinished, open-ended nature of the work and the homeless person's situation, as much as collective values, that enables workers to continue to push bureaucracy outside of traditional channels.[41] Outreach work, for all its seemingly irreconcilable dilemmas, gives hints on how to improve the way we perform public work at the margins of society. In New Haven, we saw some evidence that the multiple needs of mentally ill homeless persons propelled workers to make interventions that could lead to changes in local mental health care. It appears that a "bottom up," street-level approach, in which outreach workers respond to the demonstrated needs of their clients, may result not only in coordinated services for individual clients, but in coordination and accessibility of services for mentally ill homeless persons in general.[42]

Street-level integrating factors include embracing personal responsibility. Outreach workers witness the compounding effects of displacement and stigma that come with being homeless and mentally ill. This witnessing is a profoundly unsettling experience which generates in them a sense of urgency to help their clients. Workers fear that failure to act may mean not only untreated mental illness and a poor quality of life for homeless persons, but quite possibly victimization on the streets, untreated physical illness, and even death. The outreach team channels individual workers' passion and sense of mission into emerging clinical standards. In New Haven, passion was linked with clinical technique through the concept that workers must embrace personal responsibility for the client in the face of fragmented systems of care. Passion and personal responsibility do not, of themselves, change organizations. Rather, they seem to be driving forces behind the work and its wider influences.

Street-level work may uncover dilemmas that planners and policy makers did not anticipate in more than broad outlines. When a client population is well known, planners may be able to assess in advance the major barriers to care and the broad initiatives needed to overcome them. With this knowledge in hand, they can attempt to coordinate their efforts with those of other service providers. When the target population is homeless and mentally ill, however, the problem is not merely that of inadequate or inaccessible services but a lack of knowledge of how to help these "unknown" individuals. When this is the case, program development is likely to take place in stages that mirror the various levels of care required of a coordinated service system.

In New Haven, the sequential mastering of individual client and program tasks—learning how to find and build trust with homeless persons, how to provide clinical services, how to move clients on to continuing treatment, and how to ease the social isolation of newly housed clients—was associated with coordination of services. In the outreach phase, workers developed relationships with soup kitchen and shelter staff, teaching them how to identity the project's target population and gaining introductions from them that quickened the engagement process with prospective clients. Later, observation of clients' social isolation after they were placed in their own apartments prompted the establishment of a project to involve community and civic organizations in helping homeless persons make a successful transition to permanent housing.[43]

Assertive street outreach has its counterpart in assertive resource acquisition through "pushing and pulling" techniques. In New Haven, workers and clinical supervisors helped break down barriers to the rapid admission of clients into the community mental health center by pushing clinicians to meet their new clients (or patients) outside of the building. Outreach workers pulled referrals from unresponsive home health care agencies that actively sought to work with their clients, and directed them toward those that met their high standards. The end result of this hiring and firing was that workers began to see more flexibility from home health care agencies in general, as demonstrated by their outreach to shelters, assistance with entitlement applications, and refusal to take no for an answer from hard-to-reach individuals.

Finally, there is a Trojan horse factor. In the early stages of a homeless outreach project's development, the team may both suffer and benefit from the benign neglect of its host organization, which makes an initial commitment of resources but holds off on a long-term commitment to this unproven work. The program's relative invisibility gives it the freedom to experiment with unorthodox treatment approaches that might, with more scrutiny, prompt concerns about clinical liability which could slow implementation. Later, when the project enters the stage of transferring clients for continuing treatment, the mental health system finds that it is responsible for a new group of clients, even if it has not developed practices to accommodate it. The resulting push for systemic change is fueled in part by outreach teams that have fostered a sense of systems-wide responsibility for homeless persons. There are other encouraging aspects of work at the margins. One is outreach workers' ideal of working in partnership with the whole person. Now, it is true that the term *partnership* belies differences in power and can lend a cozy feeling to relationships that are fraught with dilemmas. Even so, the term denotes a relative shift from the workers' orchestration of services to clients' involvement in shaping their own destinies. The partnership ideal is not new to homeless outreach work: both the mental health consumer movement and proponents of recovery from mental illness[44] have been advocating for it for years. Encounters with homeless individuals on their own turf simply encourage this ideal in a particular way. The lessons of meeting people within the environment that is strangling them can infiltrate institutions and professions through the day-to-day interactions of outreach workers with their more office-bound colleagues, with the caveat that administrative support will eventually be needed to effect lasting changes in practice.

If assertive outreach work impinges upon advocacy, then there may be room for further partnerships at the margins between service providers and antihomelessness advocates. Carl Cohen and Kenneth Thompson argue that homeless mentally ill persons should be seen first as impoverished and disenfranchised rather than diseased and that mental health workers should see advocacy for basic goods and services as a central ingredient of their practice. By doing so, workers may become part of a larger constituency to address political questions of rights and equity. Programs that are open to all homeless persons, Cohen and Thompson suggest, should be considered as an alternative to those that target a disabled subset of the homeless population.[45]

There are barriers to such partnerships. Outreach programs have strong professional and organizational incentives to hoard their resources, especially during times of actual and threatened cutbacks in social services. Antihomelessness advocates are wary of being co-opted by large social service organizations, which they see as part of the problem of homelessness rather than part of the solution. And one could argue that the notion of partnership between service providers and advocates reveals a misunderstanding of their respective functions: advocates must keep their distance from mainstream institutions in order to maintain the pitch of their more radical solutions. On the other hand, one can exaggerate the differences between services and advocacy. Outreach workers are advocates for their clients, and their efforts may influence service providers, if not social and economic conditions writ large.

Cooperative efforts might be built upon the notion of homeless persons as citizens who contribute to the commonweal and deserve to share in the common benefits of mainstream life.[46] More concretely, they might include advocacy for job training and job creation—the weakest links in the range of services offered by outreach programs.[47] The harsher aspects of welfare reform and managed care affect all poor persons. Political action groups and class-action lawsuits, as well as alliances with researchers who can document the effects of such policies on the poor, might be initiated. Such efforts could be nurtured by contacts in the field between antihomelessness advocates and outreach workers. Joint grant efforts for innovative programs, written in response to federal and private funding opportunities, might provide one vehicle for such efforts.

With long-term solutions to homelessness far off, outreach work can be an important link to mainstream services and resources for the most disheartened and disturbed. Outreach work need not be limited to work with mentally ill homeless persons, if we think of it as a rescue effort with victims of social and economic disaster who have ended up at the extreme margins of society. Such programs are not cheap,[48] although costs might be reduced over time as workers establish stronger relationships with shelters, soup kitchens, and other homeless agencies, leaving only the most alienated street individuals to receive intensive outreach and engagement efforts.

One should not claim too much for these transactions. Many factors combine to thwart the work that goes on between homeless people and outreach workers. Outreach teams depend on public funding and public institutions for their continued existence, and they are situated within service systems that shape and limit their possibilities. Outreach workers continue to struggle with the irreconcilable demands of street and institution; homeless persons continue to face uncertain prospects in the housed world. But while shaped by institutional forces, boundary transactions also influence the institutions that send workers out to the margins. The degree to which they can produce lasting benefits for homeless persons awaits social and political decisions about the importance of such nontraditional efforts, and of long-term initiatives to end homelessness. The location of outreach work at the margins of society, though, presents opportunities for developing strategies that may lead to successful efforts with those who live at the margins. Just as Lipsky's street-level bureaucrats make public policy, outreach workers create the business of homelessness while negotiating from within it. This suggests that the program citizenship which workers can offer their clients at a minimum may not be an end in itself, but one route to legitimate citizenship.

And this last possibility implies the question of where social services end and "natural" community support begins. If homeless individuals are to move from clienthood to community membership, it seems reasonable to suppose they must develop positive relationships with people who are not paid to be part of their lives. Liberal thinkers and policy makers on homelessness and poverty need to fashion their own arguments for the role of "community" to counter those offered by conservative thinkers and policy makers who hold it up as the free-market answer to government-funded programs. Efforts to integrate formerly homeless persons into their neighborhoods and communities may include the collaborative work of service providers and advocates with landlords, employers, and neighborhood and municipal leaders. Creating links between newly housed people and their "informal" or "associational" sector[49] may be one way to reinvigorate community life and give formerly homeless individuals an opportunity to participate as citizens. Supported housing, including mutual self-help and the availability of social services, need not be provided through formal programs alone. Neighborhood and civic organizations may be able to help without turning their activities into formal programs.

The recovery and consumer movements, with their emphasis on self-esteem and full participation in creating one's own destiny, may provide guidance for such efforts. Meaningful work, including alternative work such as telling one's story to the public, is another route to community membership.[50] Social service institutions can contribute to community efforts while committing themselves to a relative marginalization, taking a few steps back and letting others do their part.[51] It may be, of course, that many natural associations are already taking place between formerly homeless individuals and community members and organizations, without the help of planners and policy makers. Cooperative endeavors between service providers and community organizations and individuals could teach us how these associations happen and how the lessons we learn from them can be extended.

Yet those on the mainstream side of the border, whether outreach workers, social service organizations, policy makers, or concerned citizens, remain power brokers, and the quality of self-consciousness or reflexivity that I discussed earlier is critical. "Whose citizenship?" and "For whose benefit?" are questions we need to ask ourselves as we engage in our rescue efforts. By doing so, we may be able to avoid offering homeless persons a citizenship that is only an expression of nostalgia, not one that can find a niche in our modern, disjointed communities.[52] We may be able to seriously consider the rights of others to be different, even to reject what seems to be the best definition of citizenship we can offer to the marginalized.[53] We may be able to wonder out loud whether program citizenship is a humane alternative for some severely damaged individuals. And we may use such thinking to explore whether we can maintain a collective commitment to basic human needs while allowing for permeable borders between clienthood and community membership, or between community as a whole and subcommunities of the different.[54]

6

Conclusion

We cross a foggy border of sleep to find our waking selves. An hour later our working selves greet us at the office. We encounter boundaries of self and other, of task and situation. We create and use borders as starting and stopping points for thought. We engage in brief meetings that we promptly forget and in business transactions that make or unmake our livelihoods or—in the case of doctor and patient, for example—even our lives. In performing these transactions, we come up against structures of place and institution that are more or less receptive or impervious to our personal talents. The border crossings of homeless people and outreach workers have an air of higher drama than most because they take place at what might be called the moral and psychological border of society itself.

Homelessness is, in part, a bureaucratic and political category. Its divisions by time served, demographics, disability, or the sheer bad luck of its occupants are abstractions that give order to our thinking and help us allocate scarce resources for unlimited human needs. The otherness of homelessness has its special stigmata, derived from history, from observation of homeless persons, and from our pity, disgust, and fears. We mentally place homeless individuals at our symbolic border and see them as living apart from us, perhaps because of our uncomfortable feeling of closeness to them.[1]

A few themes, beyond the theme of mental illness, gave common shape to the experiences of the homeless individuals I met. Those included a pervasive sense of negativity and alienation. The insult of society's focus on their personal deficiencies compounds the injury that homelessness brings crashing down on them. But the subjective experience of desolation is opposed by a raw struggle for existence. If many homeless individuals have lost family, friends, social support, and the jobs and status that provide an invisible buffer of good luck for the rest of us, then at least they have come face-to-face with the one necessary task— that of staying alive—and this has given them a keen eye for seizing the moment.

The outreach worker's dilemma is not new. The ideal of individual care and the reality of mass-produced units of work thread through the activities of other public workers. Yet outreach workers jealously defend and create their uniqueness. They reverse the usual protocol of office-bound work by going out to enlist individuals who are not seeking their help. They wrestle with the contradictory demands of homeless individuals and social service institutions. They believe that connection with a caring human being, not tangible resources alone, is needed to pull people out of a sea of negativity. They recognize that they must shape the homeless person as a client to meet the requirements of other agencies. And they must do so quickly in order to move on to the next person in line. Even when they are able to deliver the services they promise, they must wonder whether their clients will attain more than a second-class citizenship in mainstream society.

Boundary encounters involve negotiations over the tangible goods of housing, jobs, and income support, and the intangible goods of reconnection to family, identity as a housed person, and a sense of belonging in the mainstream community. Homeless persons may distrust outreach workers who represent institutions that labeled or confined them when they were among the barely housed. They may have a mental illness that distorts their appraisal of workers, or a simple mistrust of others' intentions that has served them well on the streets. They sometimes have unrealistic fantasies of the housed life, but they may also recount their fantasies in order to remind workers that they too have dreams and they too deserve the comforts of home and companionship. They calculate the clienthood and marginal mainstream identity with which they will pay for housing. To those who miss the context in which it is given, their refusal of the worker's generous offer is a confirmation of their illness or incompetence.[2]

Workers undergo an identity crisis as well. Their exposure to extreme poverty at the margins arouses in them conflicting emotions of outrage and pity, revulsion and the wish to flee. In becoming something like homeless persons in order to get close to them, they experience a psychological homelessness that can sharpen their skills or drive them into the back rooms of soup kitchens. As if in compensation for the starkness of their encounters, they are given a set of tasks and resources that orients them in a professional world far from the streets. If tangible resources are the tools that workers use to maintain a professional identity on the streets, the outreach team is the mediating force between workers and social service institutions. The team attempts to minimize institutional barriers and justify to outreach workers the work they are doing. It helps workers to manage the compromises of their practice by placing the work within a transcendent context of equity and the homeless individual's right to full citizenship.

Boundary encounters point beyond outreach teams to the institutions that sponsor them. Public human service organizations maintain simultaneous allegiance to their clients and to their own survival. Funding requirements to justify the cost of services, research requirements to reach statistical significance, and institutional tendencies to mass-produce solutions and clients push caseloads to the point where consistent individual care becomes almost impossible to achieve. Categorical funding for homeless services, flowing from the economic reality of limited resources and shifting determinations of need and merit, simultaneously makes the work manageable and threatens to diminish the spirit in which it is undertaken.

The passage from street to housing is a perilous one for homeless persons; the dilemma of human service work is exhausting for outreach workers. But the other side of peril is opportunity. Outreach work spans a series of encounters that host a series of crises in the homeless person's movement from homelessness to home. These crises, in turn, host dilemmas and opportunities for homeless individuals, outreach workers, and their institutions. Meetings between homeless individuals and outreach workers, then, create openings for a different kind of work with the marginalized and for modifying institutional practice.

If boundary encounters imply questions about how far rescue efforts should go and what social contribution we should expect from the rescued in exchange for these efforts, then other questions follow. How do we balance the issues of what is right and just with issues of cost? What results are even possible? Boundary encounters engage these questions by their location at the point where society's reach ends and a frontier of exclusion begins. They are partly defined by the way in which these questions tug at them, leaving workers with hopes that go beyond the usual limits of social work and with nagging fears that they may not be able to relieve the suffering of more than a few individuals.

Early in this report, I used the metaphor of a web to describe a study that would be centered on face-to-face encounters. Those encounters were the center of the web, with filaments stretching out on either side of a border separating homeless individuals and outreach workers. This metaphor will serve me again for some concluding thoughts. One could say that boundary encounters lie at the outer edge of a web whose center is society and its institutions. Using this perspective, we can refer the implications of encounters at the margins to the public that pays for them and the social and institutional mechanisms which start and stop the efforts of outreach workers.

There is a national debate about the cost of poverty programs. Plans are being floated to privatize some programs, and managed care is the new panacea for containing health costs in the public as well as private sectors. Time limits for income-support programs are in place in many states. But regardless of a shift toward a reduced role for government, public institutions and private agencies doing public work will continue to loom large in our approaches to poverty and homelessness, as avenues of resource opportunity on the one hand and of containment of the poor on the other. Through our responses to homelessness, we are asking and answering our own questions about where to locate our social boundary. But perhaps we have reached a critical juncture in our collective thinking. We now seem to accept deep poverty and the notion that we no longer have the capacity or moral obligation to stop the drift of millions more into it. Or perhaps, as a recent national survey indicates, our response to homelessness is more complicated than that: we favor social programs but also support punitive measures to reduce the public visibility of homeless people. It seems that our public will is diffuse and can be pushed in one direction or the other by politicians and policy makers.[3] With the right combinations of advocacy on either side, we might fashion either a new vision of social justice or new institutional techniques to exclude the poor and decrease their public visibility. In the latter case, new and negative interpretations of the right to a minimal standard of living for those we are tempted to define as unsalvageable might be put forth.

We should not assume that the measure of our acceptance of deep poverty will come only through the number of programs we eliminate. Cuts in funding could contribute to a rise in homelessness and prompt a new wave of services. But such programs could be asked, in effect, to help advance policies that increase rather than reduce social and economic separation. The specifics would vary, but the basic mode could be that of spending enough money to keep most people alive while creating a permanent marginal population of those whom we have concluded will never make it in mainstream society. Soup kitchens and shelters might prosper but become ever less visible in ever more restricted urban damage zones. As public visibility of homeless persons decreases and the notion of rugged individual responsibility for one's lot in life speaks with the loudest voice, emergency relief programs would become long-term "solutions." Marginal persons would live in poverty maintenance zones while the issues of jobs and housing were kept off the public policy table. Along with these trends, there would be a more subtle dimming of vision. There is a psychological and institutional routinization that allows us to keep going and maintain hope for our own prospects while being quietly troubled, but ever less so, by the sight of people at the margins. Jack London observed this normalization of disaster in another country almost a hundred years ago when he wrote that "the people of England have come to look upon starvation and suffering . . . as part of the social order."[4]

This report owes much to the tensions between street work and institutional immobility, program citizenship and legitimate citizenship, and categorical programs and unique individuals. Those tensions, even when provisionally resolved, reveal others. Encounters at the margins make us question our most deeply held beliefs about society and human nature by exposing their fault lines and showing us how we patch and paste together our ideals to fit the circumstances of our everyday lives. Sooner or later, we come face-to-face with our ambivalence about the ideals that we take to the margins. Sooner or later, outreach workers confront a case that confounds all their efforts. The homeless man with severe mental illness, a fitting object of compassion, is also a chronic alcoholic with no intention or willpower to stop drinking. Workers help him anyway. After endless hours of filling out applications and making phone calls, they learn that although he immigrated, it appears legally, to the United States some years ago, he never followed through on an application for citizenship and thus is not eligible for any form of public or local assistance. Perhaps the man did not understand or remember his legal status. Years of drinking, untreated mental illness, and homelessness have muddled his identity for him. Still, workers may wonder about his truthfulness. But they call in a favor from a landlord who has housed many of their clients. Then, as if mocking their insistence on helping him, the man, after years of surviving on the streets, becomes physically ill, but treatment is ineffective because doctors are unable to diagnose his condition. He receives medical care from a local health clinic and accumulates a mountain of bills that will never be paid. During testing, it is discovered that he suffered brain trauma at some point in his life. Perhaps this is the reason he wanders the rooming house at night, occasionally urinating and defecating in the hallways. He is not deemed psychiatrically disabled enough to be hospitalized in the one public inpatient unit that might accept him. No hospital will take him in for exploratory surgery and further lab tests that might lead to a firmer diagnosis and treatment of his physical ailments. His landlord says he has to go before the smell of urine and feces drives out the rest of his tenants. No nursing facility will accept him because he cannot pay. At this point, workers, like those who would not have chosen to pay for programs to find such individuals in the first place, may wonder whether there are rational limits to help, even in a compassionate society. Their desire to assimilate help may turn to a desire to coerce better behavior or turn away the supplicant.[5]

Hard cases may make for bad public policy, but they make for good tests of values that are rarely challenged to the utmost. In this sense, boundary encounters do society a service. They force us to discover what we mean when we talk about citizenship and justice. And at the risk of letting society and public institutions off the hook at the last moment, they also remind us that there are limits to what our caring and programs can do for others. There are blows from which people cannot recover, and lines of separation that they and we cannot cross. Yet even so, the efforts we do make are one stream of influence that will inform our policies and programs, and our working definitions of the rights and responsibilities of membership in society.

Notes

PREFACE

1. Richard Tessler and Deborah Dennis estimate the prevalence of mental illness at about one-third; see Tessler and Dennis, *A Synthesis of NIMH-Funded Research Concerning Persons Who Are Homeless and Mentally Ill* (Rockville, Md.: National Institute of Mental Health, 1989). Paul Koegel, Audrey Burnham, and Jim Baumohl, using schizophrenia and affective disorders as the standard, estimate a 20 to 23 percent rate of "severe and disabling" mental illness, in their essay The Causes of Homelessness, in *Homelessness in America,* ed. J. Baumohl (Phoenix: Oryx Press, 1996), 24–33.

2. Tessler and Dennis 1989.

3. R. E. Drake, F. C. Osher, and M. A. Wallach, Homelessness and Dual Diagnosis, *American Psychologist* 46, no. 11 (November 1991), 1149–1158. For more about research on mental illness and substance abuse among the homeless, see P. J. Fischer and W. R. Breakey, The Epidemiology of Alcohol, Drug, and Mental Disorders among Homeless Persons, *American Psychologist* 46, no. 11 (November 1991), 1115–1128. Many studies of prevalence rates of mental illness, substance abuse, and alcoholism among the homeless population are limited by the use of lifetime prevalence or cross-sectional data, by disagreements on how to define homelessness or mental illness, or by focusing only on single homeless persons, among other problems.

4. M. Rowe, M. A. Hoge, and D. Fisk, Critical Issues in Serving People Who Are Homeless and Mentally Ill, *Administration and Policy in Mental Health* 23, no. 6 (July 1996), 555–565; M. Rowe, M. A. Hoge, and D. Fisk, The Man with the Bright Yellow Sneakers: A Case Example of Assertive Outreach to Mentally Ill Homeless Persons, *Continuum: Developments in Ambulatory Health Care* 3, no. 4 (winter 1996), 265–268; M. Rowe, M. A. Hoge, and D. Fisk, Who Cares for Mentally Ill Homeless People?: Individual, Social, and Mental Health System Perspectives, *Continuum: Developments in Ambulatory Health Care* 3,

no. 4 (winter 1996), 257–264; M. Rowe, M. A. Hoge, and D. Fisk, Services for Mentally Ill Homeless Persons: Street-Level Integration, *American Journal of Orthopsychiatry* 68, no. 3 (1998), 490–496; and D. Laub and M. Rowe, Witnessing Homelessness (manuscript, 1998).

CHAPTER 1. INTRODUCTION

1. K. Hopper, Regulation from Without: The Shadow Side of Coercion, in *Coercion and Aggressive Community Treatment: A New Frontier in Mental Health Law,* ed. D. L. Dennis and J. Monahan (New York: Plenum Press, 1996), 197–212, at 197.

2. For an alternative view, see P. Marin, Helping and Hating the Homeless, *Harper's,* January 1987, 39–49. See also a discussion of this article in K. Hopper and J. Baumohl, Held in Abeyance: Rethinking Homelessness and Advocacy, *American Behavioral Scientist* 37, no. 4 (February 1994), 522–552.

3. See P. H. Rossi, *Down and Out In America: The Origins of Homelessness* (Chicago: University of Chicago Press, 1989). See also E. L. Bassuk and D. Franklin, Homelessness Past and Present: The Case of the United States, 1890–1925, *New England Journal of Public Policy* 8, no. 1 (spring-summer 1992), 67–84. Kai Erikson supplied the term "barely housed."

4. J. M. Townsend, Stereotypes of Mental Illness: A Comparison with Ethnic Stereotypes, *Culture, Medicine, and Psychiatry* 3 (1979), 205–229.

5. M. Ignatieff, *The Needs of Strangers* (London: Chatto & Windus, Hogarth Press, 1984).

6. M. Douglas, *Purity and Danger: An Analysis of Concepts of Pollution and Taboo* (Boston: Routledge and Kegan Paul, 1976).

7. E. Goffman, *The Presentation of Self in Everyday Life* (Garden City, N.Y.: Doubleday, 1959), 235. See also Michel Foucault's discussion of reason's historical defeat (versus understanding) of madness in *Madness and Civilization: A History of Insanity in the Age of Reason* (New York: Pantheon, 1965).

8. See J. R. Belcher, Rights versus Needs of Homeless Mentally Ill Persons, *Social Work* (September-October 1988), 398–402.

9. See Anne Lovell's discussion of street and organizational time and the differences in power associated with each, in her essay Seizing the Moment: Power, Contingency, and Temporality in Street Life, in *The Politics of Time,* ed. H. J. Rutz, American Anthropological Society Monograph Series, no 4 (Washington, D.C.: American Anthropological Society, 1992), 86–107.

10. From his comments on an earlier draft of this study.

11. See Elliot Liebow's comments on the researcher as a research instrument in *Tell Them Who I Am: The Lives of Homeless Women* (New York: Free Press, 1993).

12. P. Rabinow, *Reflections on Field Work in Morocco* (Berkeley: University of California Press, 1977).

CHAPTER 2. HOMELESS PEOPLE

1. W. K. Taub and L. Sawyers, *Marxism and the Metropolis: New Perspectives in Urban Political Economy* (New York: Oxford University Press, 1978).

2. Sal Brancati, then director of Administrative Services for the city of New Haven, provided this information at a June 1992 Opportunities Industrialization Center conference.

3. Tomas Reyes (president of the New Haven Board of Aldermen), interview by author, New Haven, Conn., 1995.

4. See W. Finnegan, A Reporter at Large, parts 1 and 2, *New Yorker,* 10 September 1990, 51–86; 17 September 1990, 60–90.

5. D. L. Dennis, J. C. Buckner, F. R. Lipton, and I. S. Levine, A Decade of Research and Services for Homeless Mentally Ill Persons: Where Do We Stand?, *American Psychologist* 46, no. 11 (November 1991), 1129–1138.

6. R. I. Jahiel, Homeless-Making Processes and the Homeless Makers, in *Homelessness: A Person-Oriented Approach,* ed. R. I. Jahiel (Baltimore: Johns Hopkins University Press, 1992), 269–296.

7. J. Kozol, *Rachel and Her Children: Homeless Families in America* (New York: Ballantine Books, 1988).

8. K. Hopper, More than Passing Strange: Homelessness and Mental Illness in New York City, *American Ethnologist* 15, no. 1 (February 1988), 155–167.

9. D. Mossman and M. I. Perlin, Psychiatry and the Homeless: A Reply to Dr. Lamb, *American Journal of Psychiatry* 149, no. 7 (July 1992), 951–957; P. Rossi, *Without Shelter: Homelessness in the 1980s* (New York: Priority Press, 1989).

10. M. Foscarinis, The Politics of Homelessness: A Call to Action, *American Psychologist* 46, no. 11 (November 1991), 1232–1238.

11. M. R. Burt, *Over the Edge: The Growth of Homelessness in the 1980s* (New York: Russell Sage Foundation, 1992). See also Rossi 1989b.

12. Hopper 1988, 160.

13. This information comes from my work with city officials at that time.

14. P. Koegel, A. Burnham, and R. K. Farr, Subsistence Adaptation among Homeless Adults in the Inner City of Los Angeles, *Journal of Social Issues* 46, no. 4 (1990), 83–107. See also G. A. Dordick, *Something Left to Lose: Personal Relations and Survival among New York's Homeless* (Philadelphia: Temple University Press, 1997); and D. A. Snow, L. Anderson, T. Quist, and D. Cress, Material Survival Strategies on the Street: Homeless People as Bricoleurs, in *Homelessness in America,* ed. J. Baumohl (Phoenix: Oryx Press, 1996), 86–96. Snow and his colleagues describe homeless people as "bricoleurs" who devise "unconventional but pragmatic solutions (*bricolages*) to pressing problems" using "whatever means are at their disposal" (93).

15. Lovell 1992.

16. A. M. Lovell and S. Cohn, The Elaboration of "Choice" in a Program for Persons Labeled Psychiatrically Disabled, *Human Organization* 57, no. 1 (spring 1998), 8–20.

17. R. Rosenthal, *Homeless in Paradise: A Map of the Terrain* (Philadelphia: Temple University Press, 1994). See also D. A. Snow and L. Anderson, *Down on Their Luck: A Study of Homeless Street People* (Berkeley: University of California Press, 1993); and Koegel, Burnham, and Farr 1988.

18. Lovell 1992.

19. G. Orwell, *Down and Out in Paris and London* (New York: Harcourt Brace Jovanovich, 1933), 129.

20. See Dordick 1997 on a concern for reciprocity among homeless persons.

21. The words I attribute to an informant are the words he or she actually spoke. I have edited out many of the repetitions that go unnoticed in everyday conversation but are distracting in print. In a few cases I have also reordered sentences to clarify the meaning of a passage.

22. Snow and Anderson 1993.

23. Burt 1992.

24. See E. L. Bassuk, The Homelessness Problem, *Scientific American* 251, no. 1 (July 1984), 40–45. See also E. Baxter and K. Hopper, *Private Lives/Public Spaces: Homeless Adults on the Streets of New York City* (New York: Community Service Society, 1981).

25. Acknowledging the small size of my sample, I was struck by the theme of males, especially white males, who were vulnerable to the death of the mother.

26. See Rossi 1989b.

27. D. A. Snow and L. Anderson, Identity Work among the Home-

less: The Verbal Construction and Avowal of Personal Identities, *American Journal of Sociology* 92, no. 6 (May 1987), 1336–1371.

28. See Rosenthal (1994), who argues that without more jobs that pay decent wages, and supports such as day care and transportation for those who need it, education will do little to improve the lot of the homeless poor.

29. Ibid. See also Snow and Anderson 1993.

30. K. Erikson, *A New Species of Trouble: Explorations in Disaster, Trauma, and Community* (New York: Norton, 1994), 159.

31. See N. C. Ware, R. R. Desjarlais, T. L. Avruskin, J. Breslau, B. J. Good, and S. M. Goldfinger, Empowerment and the Transition to Housing for Homeless Mentally Ill People: An Anthropological Perspective, *New England Journal of Public Policy* 8, no. 1 (spring-summer 1992), 265–280.

32. By way of contrast, see Baxter and Hopper 1981.

33. See Liebow 1993.

34. C. I. Cohen and K. S. Thompson, Psychiatry and the Homeless, *Biological Psychiatry* 32 (1992), 383–386. See also J. D. Wright, Poor People, Poor Health: The Health Status of the Homeless, *Journal of Social Issues* 46, no. 4 (1990), 49–64.

35. See Baxter and Hopper 1981.

36. For further discussions about the ways in which constant exposure to stress and physical deprivation wear away layer after layer of self-protection, see S. D. Mullins, R. Schuh, L. Thomas, K. Thompson, and J. Cyganovich, *STEPS OUT: A Peer-Integrated Outreach and Treatment Model* (Pittsburgh: n.p., 1993); and L. Goodman, L. Saxe, and M. Harvey, Homelessness as Psychological Trauma: Broadening Perspectives, *American Psychologist* 46, no. 11 (November 1991), 1219–1225.

37. Ignatieff 1984, 41.

38. Ibid., 43.

39. Snow and Anderson 1987.

40. Jacqueline Wiseman uses the term *stations* to convey the looping rounds of institutional life of skid row alcoholics in *Stations of the Lost: The Treatment of Skid-Row Alcoholics* (Englewood Cliffs, N.J.: Prentice-Hall, 1970).

41. K. Gounis and E. Susser, Shelterization and Its Implications for Mental Health Services, in *Psychiatry Takes to the Streets: Outreach and Crisis Intervention for the Mentally Ill,* ed. N. Cohen (New York: Guilford Press, 1990), 231–255.

42. See Wiseman's finding (1970) that skid row alcoholics view jail rules as an extension of their keepers' personalities.

43. Most of the criticism of shelter staff that I heard was directed toward residential aides, the least-trained and lowest-paid shelter staff, who function as the police force of shelters.

44. K. Erikson, *Everything in Its Path: Destruction of Community in the Buffalo Creek Flood* (New York: Simon and Schuster, 1976), 11.

45. Any description of homeless persons' contacts with social service and welfare agencies risks becoming dated quickly, with changes at the federal, state, and local levels constantly being considered or enacted. However, the principle that homeless persons are ill adapted to negotiating with these gatekeepers to citizenship still applies. That in the future there may be fewer and narrower such gates through which poor people can pass may only increase the frustration they already experience.

46. E. Goffman, *Stigma: Notes on the Management of Spoiled Identity* (New York: J. Aronson, 1974).

47. L. Mansouri and D. A. Dowell, Perceptions of Stigma among the Long-Term Mentally Ill, *Psychosocial Rehabilitation Journal* 13, no. 1 (July 1989), 79–91.

48. Ibid., referring to the work of Thomas J. Scheff on stigma.

49. S. E. Estroff, Self, Identity, and Subjective Experiences of Schizophrenia: In Search of the Subject, *Schizophrenia Bulletin* 15, no. 2 (1989), 189–196.

50. E. M. Gruenberg, The Social Breakdown Syndrome: Some Origins, *American Journal of Psychiatry* 123, no. 12 (June 1967), 1481–1489.

51. C. I. Barnard, *The Functions of the Executive* (Cambridge: Harvard University Press, 1938).

52. See Rosenthal 1994 on how this process affects resource gathering for homeless people.

53. Erikson 1994.

54. Ibid., 159.

55. See H. M. Bahr, *Skid Row: An Introduction to Disaffiliation* (New York: Oxford University Press, 1973). Bahr studied skid row residents of an earlier era of homelessness and found that, in order to maintain a minimum of self-esteem, men would point to their superiority over other skid row residents. The same technique sometimes brings comfort to homeless people today.

CHAPTER 3. OUTREACH
WORKERS

1. From comments by Jim Baumohl on an earlier draft of this book.

2. See P. Boyer, *Urban Masses and Moral Order in America, 1820–1920* (Cambridge: Harvard University Press, 1978). Boyer's study is the source of most of my review of the roots of outreach from the 1820s through the settlement-house movement and the Salvation Army. Here and elsewhere in this chapter I am indebted to Jim Baumohl for invaluable suggestions regarding sources as well as for his comments to me on the history of outreach work.

3. Boyer 1978, 152.

4. Baumohl, comments.

5. See I. A. Spergel, *The Youth Gang Problem: A Community Approach* (New York: Oxford University Press, 1995).

6. See M. W. Klein, *Street Gangs and Street Workers* (Englewood Cliffs, N.J.: Prentice-Hall, 1971).

7. Baumohl, comments.

8. D. L. Dennis and J. Monahan, Introduction, in *Coercion and Aggressive Community Treatment,* ed. D. L. Dennis and J. Monahan (New York: Plenum Press, 1996), 1–9.

9. S. P. Segal, J. Baumohl, and E. Johnson, Falling through the Cracks: Mental Disorder and Social Margin in a Young Vagrant Population, *Social Problems* 23, no. 3 (1977), 387–400.

10. P. Koegel, Through a Different Lens: An Anthropological Perspective on the Homeless Mentally Ill, *Culture, Medicine, and Psychiatry* 16 (1992), 1–22.

11. See S. P. Segal and J. Baumohl, Engaging the Disengaged: Proposals on Madness and Vagrancy, *Social Work* 24, no. 5 (September 1980), 358–365.

12. N. L. Cohen and L. R. Marcos, Outreach Intervention Models for the Homeless Mentally Ill, in *Treating the Homeless Mentally Ill: A Report of the Task Force on the Homeless Mentally Ill,* ed. R. H. Lamb, L. L. Bachrach, and F. I. Kass (Washington, D.C.: American Psychiatric Association, 1992), 141–157. See also R. H. Lamb, L. L. Bachrach, S. M. Goldfinger, and F. I. Kass, Summary and Recommendations, in *Treating the Homeless Mentally Ill: A Report of the Task Force on the Homeless Mentally Ill,* ed. R. H. Lamb, L. L. Bachrach, and F. I. Kass (Washington, D.C.: American Psychiatric Association, 1992), 1–10.

13. P. Ridgway, *The Voice of Consumers in Mental Health Systems: A Call for Change* (Washington, D.C.: National Institute of Mental

Health, 1988). See also L. Chafetz, Why Clinicians Distance Themselves from the Homeless Mentally Ill, in *Treating the Homeless Mentally Ill: A Report of the Task Force on the Homeless Mentally Ill,* ed. R. H. Lamb, L. L. Bachrach, and F. I. Kass (Washington, D.C.: American Psychiatric Association, 1992), 95–107; M. Martin, The Homeless Mentally Ill and Community-Based Care: Changing a Mindset, *Community Mental Health Journal* 26, no. 5 (1990), 435–447; J. V. Vaccaro, R. P. Liberman, S. Friedlob, and S. Dempsay, Challenge and Opportunity: Rehabilitating the Homeless Mentally Ill, in *Treating the Homeless Mentally Ill: A Report of the Task Force on the Homeless Mentally Ill,* ed. R. H. Lamb, L. L. Bachrach, and F. I. Kass (Washington, D.C.: American Psychiatric Association, 1992), 279–297.

14. *Reaching Out: A Guide for Service Providers* (Washington, D.C.: Interagency Council on the Homeless, 1991).

15. F. V. Swayze, Clinical Case Management with the Homeless Mentally Ill, in *Treating the Homeless Mentally Ill: A Report of the Task Force on the Homeless Mentally Ill,* ed. R. H. Lamb, L. L. Bachrach, and F. I. Kass (Washington, D.C.: American Psychiatric Association, 1992), 203–219. See also P. W. Brickner, Medical Concerns of Homeless Persons, in *Treating the Homeless Mentally Ill: A Report of the Task Force on the Homeless Mentally Ill,* ed. R. H. Lamb, L. L. Bachrach, and F. I. Kass (Washington, D.C.: American Psychiatric Association, 1992), 249–261; E. Susser, S. M. Goldfinger, and A. White, Some Clinical Approaches to the Homeless Mentally Ill, *Community Mental Health Journal* 25, no. 5 (1990), 463–480; and G. A. Morse, R. J. Calsyn, J. Miller, P. Rosenberg, L. West, and J. Gilliland, Outreach to Homeless Mentally Ill People: Conceptual and Clinical Considerations, *Community Mental Health Journal* 32, no. 3 (June 1996), 261–274.

16. N. L. Cohen and S. Tsemberis, Emergency Psychiatric Interventions on the Street, *New Directions for Mental Health Services* 52 (winter 1991), 3–16.

17. See P. Goering, J. Durbin, R. Foster, S. B. Hons, T. Babiek, and B. Lancee, Social Networks of Residents in Supportive Housing, *Community Mental Health Journal* 28, no. 3 (June 1992), 199–214.

18. See F. I. Kass, D. A. Kahn, and A. Felix, Day Treatment in a Shelter: A Setting for Assessment and Treatment, in *Treating the Homeless Mentally Ill: A Report of the Task Force on the Homeless Mentally Ill,* ed. R. H. Lamb, L. L. Bachrach, and F. I. Kass (Washington, D.C.: American Psychiatric Association, 1992), 263–277.

19. R. H. Lamb, L. L. Bachrach, and F. I. Kass, *Treating the Homeless Mentally Ill: A Report of the Task Force on the Homeless Mentally Ill* (Washington, D.C.: American Psychiatric Association, 1992).

20. M. B. Cohen, Social Work Practice with Homeless Mentally Ill People: Engaging the Client. *Social Work* 34, no. 6 (1989), 505–508.

21. See also E. Bittner, The Police on Skid-Row: A Study of Peace Keeping, *American Sociological Review* 32, no. 5 (October 1967), 699–715, for his comments on the sense of "exotic adventure" that motivated outreach activities on skid rows.

22. J. H. Shapiro, *Communities of the Alone: Working with Single Room Occupants in the City* (New York: Association Press, 1971).

23. Wiseman 1970.

24. Ibid.

25. Ibid.

CHAPTER 4. BOUNDARY TRANSACTIONS

1. S. P. Segal and J. Baumohl, The Community Living Room, *Social Case Work: The Journal of Contemporary Social Work* 66, no. 2 (February 1985), 111–116.

2. Segal, Baumohl, and Johnson 1977.

3. Ignatieff 1984.

4. Ibid., 34.

5. Ibid.

6. Ignatieff 1984.

7. Also see Rosenthal 1994 on the topic of alienation.

8. J. S. Strauss, The Person—Key to Understanding Mental Illness: Towards a New Dynamic Psychiatry, III, *British Journal of Psychiatry* 161, supp. 18 (1992), 19–26, at 23.

9. D. Laub, Engaging the Mentally Ill Patient (manuscript, n.d.).

10. Douglas 1976.

11. Ibid. See also Peter Berger, *The Sacred Canopy* (Garden City, N.Y.: Doubleday, 1967), for his idea that "marginal situations" remind us of the instability of the social world.

12. This is my loose interpretation of comments made by Dori Laub during a 1995 ACCESS staff training session.

13. H. Blumer, *Symbolic Interactionism: Perspective and Method* (Englewood Cliffs, N.J.: Prentice-Hall, 1969).

14. L. E. Blankertz, R. A. Cnaan, K. White, J. Fox, and K. Messinger, Outreach Efforts with Dually Diagnosed Homeless Persons, *Families in Society: The Journal of Contemporary Human Services,* September 1990, 387–397. See also Blumer 1969 and S. E. Estroff, *Making It Crazy: An Ethnography of Psychiatric Patients in an American Community* (Berkeley: University of California Press, 1981).

15. Estroff 1981.

16. H. Garfinkel, *Studies in Ethnomethodology* (Berkeley: University of California Press, 1961).

17. Ibid., 37.

18. E. Goffman, *Strategic Interaction* (Philadelphia: University of Pennsylvania Press, 1969), 3.

19. See Douglas 1976 for a discussion of the idea that we are uncomfortable with dirt because it represents disorder.

20. Snow and Anderson 1993. See also Rosenthal 1994.

21. Snow and Anderson 1987.

22. See K. Gounis, *The Domestication of Homelessness: The Politics of Space and Time in New York City Shelters* (Ph.D. diss., Columbia University, 1993).

23. Snow and Anderson 1993.

24. Wiseman 1970. See also Bahr 1973.

25. J. R. Gusfield, *Symbolic Crusade: Status Politics in the American Temperance Movement* (Chicago: University of Illinois Press, 1963).

26. The following is a partial list of reports or studies on housing models and strategies for mentally ill homeless persons: M. S. Hurlburt, R. L. Hough, and P. A. Wood, Effects of Substance Abuse on Housing Stability of Homeless Mentally Ill Persons in Supported Housing, *Psychiatric Services* 47, no. 7 (July 1996), 731–736; B. Dickey, O. Gonzalez, E. Lattimer, K. Powers, R. Schutt, and S. Goldfinger, Use of Mental Health Services by Formerly Homeless Adults Residing in Group and Independent Housing, *Psychiatric Services* 47, no. 2 (February 1996), 152–158; S. Goldfinger and R. K. Schutt, Housing Preferences and Perceptions of Health and Functioning among Homeless Mentally Ill Persons, *Psychiatric Services* 47, no. 4 (April 1996), 381–386; and P. J. Carling, Housing and Supports for Persons with Mental Illness: Emerging Approaches to Research and Practice, *Hospital and Community Psychiatry* 44, no. 5 (August 1993), 439–449.

27. P. Koegel, Through a Different Lens: An Anthropological Perspective on the Homeless Mentally Ill, *Culture, Medicine, and Psychiatry* 16 (1992), 1–22, at 14.

28. Wiseman 1970.

29. W. Kauffman, *Critique of Religion and Philosophy* (Princeton, N.J.: Princeton University Press, 1978).

30. J. C. Oates, Introduction, in *Had I a Hundred Months: New and Selected Stories, 1947–1983,* by W. Goyen (New York: Persea Books, 1986), vii–xii, at xi.

31. Erikson 1994, 234.

32. C. A. Seeger, Reflections on Working with the Homeless, *New Directions for Mental Health Services* 46 (summer 1990), 47–55. Seeger draws on the work of Robert Jay Lifton and Eric Olson.

33. See R. Rosenthal, Straighter from the Source: Alternative Methods of Researching Homelessness, *Urban Anthropology* 20, no. 2 (1991), 109–126. Dori Laub, M.D., and I have also written about the possibility of developing a videotape archive on homelessness; see Laub and Rowe 1998.

34. J. Baumohl, Addiction and the American Debate about Homelessness, *British Journal of Addiction* 87 (1992), 15–16.

35. C. Wright Mills, writing about sociology as an academic discipline, used the term *sociological imagination* to describe the capacity to shift perspective from the personal to the social realm; see C. W. Mills, *The Sociological Imagination* (New York: Oxford University Press, 1959).

36. See H. M. Spiro, M. G. M. Curnen, E. Peschel, and D. St. James, *Empathy and the Practice of Medicine: Beyond Pills and the Scalpel* (New Haven: Yale University Press, 1994).

37. J. Guare, *Six Degrees of Separation* (New York: Random House, 1990).

38. Wiseman 1970.

39. See A. W. Gouldner, *The Dialectic of Ideology and Technology* (New York: Oxford University Press, 1970). C. Wright Mills wrote that social workers are trained to think in terms of social situations rather than the social forces and normative values that shape them; see C. W. Mills, The Professional Ideology of Social Pathologists, *American Journal of Sociology* 49, no. 2 (September 1943), 165–180. Kim Hopper wrote that professionals tend to act upon social problems without considering how their disciplinary biases shape their view of these problems or the interventions they make to "solve" them; see K. Hopper, Deviance and Dwelling Space: Notes on the Resettlement of Homeless Persons with Drug and Alcohol Problems, *Contemporary Drug Problems,* fall 1989, 392–414.

CHAPTER 5. THE BUSINESS
OF HOMELESSNESS

1. See C. Perrow, *Complex Organizations: A Critical Essay,* 3d ed. (New York: McGraw-Hill, 1986).

2. This task force produced a report that contains the basic rationale for the ACCESS program. See *Outcasts on Main Street: Report of the Federal Task Force on Homelessness and Severe Mental Illness* (Washington, D.C.: Interagency Council on the Homeless, 1992).

3. M. Lipsky, *Street-Level Bureaucracy: Dilemmas of the Individual in Public Services* (New York: Russell Sage Foundation, 1980), 59.

4. Ignatieff 1984.

5. F. Baker, *Coordination of Alcohol, Drug Abuse, and Mental Health Services* (Rockville, Md.: Center for Substance Abuse Treatment, 1991). See also G. R. Yank and W. W. Spradin, Systems Approaches in Mental Health Administration: Linking State and Community Programs, *Administration and Policy in Mental Health* 21, no. 6 (July 1994), 463–477; and R. Agranoff, Services Integration Is Still Alive: Local Intergovernmental Bodies, *New England Journal of Human Services,* summer 1985, 16–25.

6. R. Agranoff, Human Services Integration: Past and Present Challenges in Public Administration, *Public Administration Review* 51, no. 6 (December 1991), 533–542. See also G. MacBeth, Collaboration Can Be Elusive: Virginia's Experience in Developing an Interagency System of Care, *Administration and Policy in Mental Health* 20, no. 4 (March 1993), 259–281.

7. *Services Integration: A Twenty-Year Retrospective* (Washington, D.C.: Department of Health and Human Services, 1991).

8. R. L. Warren, S. Rose, and A. F. Bergunder, *The Structure of Urban Reform* (Lexington, Mass: Lexington Books, 1974).

9. R. L. Warren, Comprehensive Planning and Coordination: Some Functional Aspects, *Social Problems* 2, no. 3 (winter 1973), 355–364.

10. Ibid. See also J. Weiss, Substance versus Symbol in Administrative Reform: The Case of Human Services Coordination, *Policy Analysis* 7, no. 2 (1981), 21–45.

11. Warren 1973.

12. See Rowe, Hoge, and Fisk 1996a.

13. Lipsky 1980.

14. Ibid., 59.

15. Ibid.

16. S. E. Estroff, Medicalizing the Margins: On Being Disgraced, Disordered, and Deserving, *Psychosocial Rehabilitation Journal* 8, no. 4 (April 1985), 34–39. See also D. A. Snow, S. G. Baker, L. Anderson, and M. Martin, The Myth of Pervasive Mental Illness among the Homeless, *Social Problems* 33, no. 5 (June 1986), 407–423.

17. Cohen and Thompson 1992a.

18. Wright, J. D.,The Mentally Ill Homeless: What Is Myth and What Is Fact?, *Social Problems* 35, no. 2 (April 1988), 182–191.

19. Lovell 1992.

20. H. H. Goldman and J. P. Morrissey, The Alchemy of Mental

Health Policy: Homelessness and the Fourth Cycle of Reform, *American Journal of Public Health* 75, no. 7 (July 1985), 727–731.

21. Lipsky 1980.

22. Estroff 1981.

23. Lipsky 1980.

24. Ibid.

25. Ibid.

26. See Liebow 1993 and Spergel 1995.

27. Chafetz 1992. See also N. L. Cohen, Stigma Is in the Eye of the Beholder: A Hospital Outreach Program for Treating Homeless Mentally Ill People, *Bulletin of the Menninger Clinic* 54, no. 2 (1990), 225–228; Wiseman 1970 on how workers psychologically insulate themselves for their emotional survival; Snow and Anderson 1993 on workers' focus on individual "ailments" in the face of their inability to affect socioeconomic factors; and Shapiro 1971 on how workers' attempts to resocialize SRO dwellers backfired because of the workers' limited focus and resources.

28. Lipsky 1980.

29. Dori Laub, M.D., and Deborah Fisk, M.S.W., developed this concept through their work as attending psychiatrist and clinical coordinator, respectively, with the New Haven ACCESS project.

30. Lipsky 1980.

31. This case vignette is based largely on material supplied to me by several outreach workers with the New Haven ACCESS project.

32. E. Durkheim, *The Elementary Forms of Religious Life* (New York: Free Press, 1965).

33. See Rowe, Hoge, and Fisk 1996a.

34. B. M. Berger, *The Survival of a Counterculture: Ideological Work and Everyday Life among Rural Communards* (Berkeley: University of California Press, 1981).

35. Baxter and Hopper 1981, 106.

36. Hopper and Baumohl 1994.

37. See Wiseman 1970.

38. J. Keck, Responding to Consumer Housing Preferences: The Toledo Experience, *Psychosocial Rehabilitation Journal* 13, no. 4 (April 1990), 51–58. See also P. Goering, J. Durbin, J. Trainor, and D. Paduchak, Developing Housing for the Homeless, *Psychosocial Rehabilitation Journal* 13, no. 4 (April 1990), 33–42; and P. J. Carling, Major Mental Illness, Housing, and Supports: The Promise of Community Integration, *American Psychologist* 45, no. 8 (August 1990), 969–975.

39. See Keck 1990. See also Carling 1993.

40. P. Ridgway, A. Simpson, F. Wittman, and G. Wheeler, Home-making and Community Building: Notes on Empowerment in Place, *Journal of Mental Health Administration* 21, no. 4 (1994), 407–418.

41. The idea of the unfinished nature of the work is based on comments by Deborah Fisk.

42. See Rowe, Hoge, and Fisk 1997.

43. The Melville Charitable Trust funded this project, called Citizens, through Columbus House Emergency Shelter.

44. L. Davidson and J. S. Strauss, Sense of Self in Recovery from Mental Illness, *British Journal of Medical Psychology* 65 (1992), 131–145.

45. C. I. Cohen and K. S. Thompson, Homeless Mentally Ill or Mentally Ill Homeless? *American Journal of Psychiatry* 149, no. 6 (1992), 812–823.

46. See R. Rosenthal, Dilemmas of Local Antihomelessness Movements, in *Homelessness in America,* ed. J. Baumohl (Phoenix: Oryx Press, 1996), 201–212.

47. Hopper and Baumohl (1994), and Rosenthal (1994), emphasize the need for employment as well as housing to pull people out of homelessness.

48. R. Rosenheck, P. Gallup, and L. K. Frisman, Health Care Utilization Costs after Entry into an Outreach Program for Homeless Mentally Ill Veterans, *Hospital and Community Psychiatry* 44, no. 2 (December 1993), 1166–1171.

49. See J. L. McKnight, Regenerating Community, *Social Policy,* winter 1987, 54–58.

50. J. Baumohl, Hope Needs Work: Picking Up from Hopper and Hawks, *British Journal of Addiction* 87 (1992), 7–8.

51. See J. L. McKnight, Redefining Community, *Self-Help and Politics,* fall-winter 1992, 56–62. McKnight writes about how "community services" can actively prevent their clients' involvement in their communities.

52. See Ignatieff 1984.

53. See J. P. Spradley, *You Owe Yourself a Drunk: An Ethnography of Urban Nomads.* (Boston: Little, Brown and Company, 1970).

54. Kim Hopper and Jim Baumohl, while not offering them as a solution to the problem of homelessness, write about the possibility of having "urban enclaves" where the stricter demands of social order are relaxed for some marginal groups; see Hopper and Baumohl 1994.

CHAPTER 6. CONCLUSION

1. K. Hopper, A Poor Apart: The Distancing of Homeless Men in New York's History, *Social Research* 58, no. 1 (spring 1991), 107–132, at 110.

2. Koegel 1992.

3. B. G. Link, S. Schwartz, R. Moore, J. Phelan, E. Struening, A. Stueve, and M. E. Colton, Public Knowledge, Attitudes, and Beliefs about Homeless People: Evidence for Compassion Fatigue? *American Journal of Community Psychology* 23, no. 4 (1995), 533–555.

4. London, J., *The People of the Abyss* (New York: Joseph Simon, 1980).

5. See Gusfield 1963. Gusfield, in his study of the American temperance movement, characterizes social reform movements as either coercive or assimilative. In coercive reform, the objects of reform are seen as rejecting reformers' values and as unwilling to change. Coercive reform, he argues, arises as a reaction to declining cultural dominance. Assimilative reformers are more sympathetic to the objects of their reform, and critical of social and economic conditions that contribute to the condition requiring reform. Gusfield talks about three forms of assimilative reform under the umbrella of social Christianity. Conservative social Christianity accepts principles of individualistic laissez-faire economy. Radical social Christianity uses religious doctrine as the foundation for an attack on the existing social and economic order. Progressive social Christianity adopts an intermediate position which is perhaps closest to that of outreach workers. All three forms are a response of the educated middle class to the suffering of others, and contain middle-class assumptions about proper outcomes for the objects of reform.

Bibliography

Agranoff, R. 1985. Services Integration Is Still Alive: Local Intergovernmental Bodies. *New England Journal of Human Services,* summer, 16–25.

———. 1991. Human Services Integration: Past and Present Challenges in Public Administration. *Public Administration Review* 51, no. 6 (December), 533–542.

Bahr, H. M. 1973. *Skid Row: An Introduction to Disaffiliation.* New York: Oxford University Press.

Baker, F. 1991. *Coordination of Alcohol, Drug Abuse, and Mental Health Services.* Rockville, Md.: Center for Substance Abuse Treatment.

Barnard, C. I. 1938. *The Functions of the Executive.* Cambridge: Harvard University Press.

Bassuk, E. L. 1984. The Homelessness Problem. *Scientific American* 251, no. 1 (July), 40–45.

Bassuk, E. L., and D. Franklin. 1992. Homelessness Past and Present: The Case of the United States, 1890–1925. *New England Journal of Public Policy* 8, no. 1 (spring-summer), 67–84.

Baumohl, J. 1992a. Addiction and the American Debate about Homelessness. *British Journal of Addiction* 87, 15–16.

———. 1992b. Hope Needs Work: Picking Up from Hopper and Hawks. *British Journal of Addiction* 87, 7–8.

———, ed. 1996. *Homelessness in America.* Phoenix: Oryx Press.

Baxter, E., and K. Hopper. 1981. *Private Lives/Public Spaces: Homeless Adults on the Streets of New York City.* New York: Community Service Society.

Belcher, J. R. 1988. Rights versus Needs of Homeless Mentally Ill Persons. *Social Work,* September-October, 399–402.

Berger, B. M. 1981. *The Survival of a Counterculture: Ideological Work and Everyday Life among Rural Communards.* Berkeley: University of California Press.

Berger, P. L. 1967. *The Sacred Canopy.* Garden City, N.Y.: Doubleday.

Bittner, E. 1967. The Police on Skid-Row: A Study of Peace Keeping. *American Psychological Review* 32, no. 5 (October), 699–715.

Blankertz, L. E., R. A. Cnaan, K. White, J. Fox, and K. Messinger. 1990. Outreach Efforts with Dually Diagnosed Homeless Persons. *Families in Society: The Journal of Contemporary Human Services,* September, 387–397.

Blumer, H. 1969. *Symbolic Interactionism: Perspective and Method.* Englewood Cliffs, N.J.: Prentice-Hall.

Boyer, P. 1978. *Urban Masses and Moral Order in America, 1820–1920.* Cambridge: Harvard University Press.

Brickner, P. W. 1992. Medical Concerns of Homeless Persons. In *Treating the Homeless Mentally Ill: A Report of the Task Force on the Homeless Mentally Ill,* ed. R. H. Lamb, L. L. Bachrach, and F. I. Kass, 249–261. Washington, D.C.: American Psychiatric Association.

Burt, M. R. 1992. *Over the Edge: The Growth of Homelessness in the 1980s.* New York: Russell Sage Foundation.

Carling, P. J. 1990. Major Mental Illness, Housing, and Supports: The Promise of Community Integration. *American Psychologist* 45, no. 8 (August), 969–975.

———. 1993. Housing and Supports for Persons with Mental Illness: Emerging Approaches to Research and Practice. *Hospital and Community Psychiatry* 44, no. 5 (August), 439–449.

Chafetz, L. 1992. Why Clinicians Distance Themselves from the Homeless Mentally Ill. In *Treating the Homeless Mentally Ill: A Report of the Task Force on the Homeless Mentally Ill,* ed. R. H. Lamb, L. L. Bachrach, and F. I. Kass, 95–107. Washington, D.C.: American Psychiatric Association.

Cohen, C. I., and K. S. Thompson. 1992a. Homeless Mentally Ill or Mentally Ill Homeless? *American Journal of Psychiatry* 149, no. 6, 812–823.

———. 1992b. Psychiatry and the Homeless. *Biological Psychiatry* 32, 383–386.

Cohen, M. B. 1989. Social Work Practice with Homeless Mentally Ill People: Engaging the Client. *Social Work* 34, no. 6, 505–508.

Cohen, N. L. 1990. Stigma Is in the Eye of the Beholder: A Hospital Outreach Program for Treating Homeless Mentally Ill People. *Bulletin of the Menninger Clinic* 54, no. 2, 225–228.

Cohen, N. L., and L. R. Marcos. 1992. Outreach Intervention Models for the Homeless Mentally Ill. In *Treating the Homeless Mentally Ill: A Report of the Task Force on the Homeless Mentally Ill,* ed. R. H. Lamb, L. L. Bachrach, and F. I. Kass, 141–157. Washington, D.C.: American Psychiatric Association.

Cohen, N. L., and S. Tsemberis. 1991. Emergency Psychiatric Interventions on the Street. *New Directions for Mental Health Services* 52 (winter), 3–16.

Davidson, L., and J. S. Strauss. 1992. Sense of Self in Recovery from Mental Illness. *British Journal of Medical Psychology* 65, 131–145.

Dennis, D. L., J. C. Buckner, F. R. Lipton, and I. S. Levine. 1991. A Decade of Research and Services for Homeless Mentally Ill Persons: Where Do We Stand? *American Psychologist* 46, no. 11 (November), 1129–1138.

Dennis, D. L., and J. Monahan. 1996a. Introduction. In *Coercion and Aggressive Community Treatment,* ed. D. L. Dennis and J. Monahan. New York: Plenum Press.

———, eds. 1996b. *Coercion and Aggressive Community Treatment.* New York: Plenum Press.

Dickey, B., O. Gonzalez, E. Lattimer, K. Powers, R. Schutt, and S. Goldfinger. 1996. Use of Mental Health Services by Formerly Homeless Adults Residing in Group and Independent Housing. *Psychiatric Services* 47, no. 2 (February), 152–158.

Dordick, G. A. 1997. Something Left to Lose: Personal Relations and Survival among New York's Homeless. Philadelphia: Temple University Press.

Douglas, M. 1976. *Purity and Danger: An Analysis of Concepts of Pollution and Taboo.* Boston: Routledge and Kegan Paul.

Drake, R. E., F. C. Osher, and M. A. Wallach. 1991. Homeless and Dual Diagnosis. *American Psychologist* 46, no. 11 (November), 1149–1158.

Durkheim, E. 1965. *The Elementary Forms of Religious Life.* New York: Free Press.

Erikson, K. 1976. *Everything in Its Path: Destruction of Community in the Buffalo Creek Flood.* New York: Simon and Schuster.

———. 1994. *A New Species of Trouble: Explorations in Disaster, Trauma, and Community.* New York: Norton.

Estroff, S. E. 1981. *Making It Crazy: An Ethnography of Psychiatric Patients in an American Community.* Berkeley: University of California Press.

———. 1989. Self, Identity, and Subjective Experiences of Schizophrenia: In Search of the Subject. *Schizophrenia Bulletin* 15, no. 2, 189–196.

———. 1995. Medicalizing the Margins: On Being Disgraced, Disordered, and Deserving. *Psychosocial Rehabilitation Journal* 8, no. 4 (April), 34–39.

Finnegan, W. 1990. A Reporter at Large. Parts 1 and 2. *New Yorker,* September 10, 51–86; September 17, 60–90.

Fischer, P. J., and W. R. Breakey. 1991. The Epidemiology of Alcohol, Drug, and Mental Disorders among Homeless Persons. *American Psychologist* 46, no. 11 (November), 1115–1128.

Foscarinis, M. 1991. The Politics of Homelessness: A Call to Action. *American Psychologist* 46, no. 11 (November), 1232–1238.

Foucault, M. 1965. *Madness and Civilization: A History of Insanity in the Age of Reason.* New York: Pantheon.

Garfinkel, H. 1961. *Studies in Ethnomethodology.* Berkeley: University of California Press.

Goering, P., J. Durbin, R. Foster, S. B. Hons, T. Babiek, and B. Lancee. 1992. Social Networks of Residents in Supportive Housing. *Community Mental Health Journal* 28, no. 3 (June), 199–214.

Goering, P., J. Durbin, J. Trainor, and D. Paduchak. 1990. Developing Housing for the Homeless. *Psychosocial Rehabilitation Journal* 13, no. 4 (April), 33–42.

Goffman, E. 1959. *The Presentation of Self in Everyday Life.* Garden City, N.Y.: Doubleday.

———. 1969. *Strategic Interaction.* Philadelphia: University of Pennsylvania Press.

———. 1974. *Stigma: Notes on the Management of Spoiled Identity.* New York: J. Aronson.

Goldfinger, S., and R. K. Schutt. 1996. Housing Preferences and Perceptions of Health and Functioning among Homeless Mentally Ill Persons. *Psychiatric Services* 47, no. 4 (April), 381–386

Goldman, H. H. and J. P. Morrissey. 1985. The Alchemy of Mental Health Policy: Homelessness and the Fourth Cycle of Reform. *American Journal of Public Health* 75, no. 7 (July), 727–731.

Goodman, L. L. Saxe, and M. Harvey. 1991. Homelessness as Psychological Trauma: Broadening Perspectives. *American Psychologist* 46, no. 11 (November), 1219–1225.

Gouldner, A. W. 1976. *The Dialectic of Ideology and Technology.* New York: Oxford University Press.

Gounis, K. 1993. *The Domestication of Homelessness: The Politics of Space and Time in New York City Shelters.* Ph.D. diss., Columbia University.

Gounis, K., and E. Susser. 1990. Shelterization and Its Implications for Mental Health Services. In *Psychiatry Takes to the Streets: Outreach and Crisis Intervention for the Mentally Ill,* ed. N. Cohen, 231–255. New York: Guilford Press.

Gruenberg, E. M. 1967. The Social Breakdown Syndrome: Some Origins. *American Journal of Psychiatry* 123, no. 12 (June), 1481–1489.

Guare, J. 1990. *Six Degrees of Separation.* New York: Random House.

Gusfield, J. R. 1963. *Symbolic Crusade: Status Politics in the American Temperance Movement.* Chicago: University of Illinois Press.

Hopper, K. 1988. More Than Passing Strange: Homelessness and Mental Illness in New York City. *American Ethnologist* 15, no. 1 (February), 155–167.

———. 1989. Deviance and Dwelling Space: Notes on the Resettlement of Homeless Persons with Drug and Alcohol Problems. *Contemporary Drug Problems,* fall, 392–414.

———. 1991. A Poor Apart: The Distancing of Homeless Men in New York's History. *Social Research* 58, no. 1 (spring), 107–132.

———. 1996. Regulation from Without: The Shadow Side of Coercion. In *Coercion and Aggressive Community Treatment: A New Frontier in Mental Health Law,* ed. D. L. Dennis and J. Monahan, 197–212. New York: Plenum Press.

Hopper, K., and J. Baumohl. 1994. Held in Abeyance: Rethinking Homelessness and Advocacy. *American Behavioral Scientist* 37, no. 4 (February), 522–552.

Hurlburt, M. S., R. L. Hough, and P. A. Wood. 1996. Effects of Substance Abuse on Housing Stability of Homeless Mentally Ill Persons in Supported Housing. *Psychiatric Services* 47, no. 7 (July), 731–736

Ignatieff, M. 1984. *The Needs of Strangers.* London: Chatto & Windus, Hogarth Press.

Jahiel, R. I. 1992a. Homeless-Making Processes and the Homeless Makers. In *Homelessness: A Prevention-Oriented Approach,* ed. R. I. Jahiel, 269–296. Baltimore: Johns Hopkins University Press.

———, ed. 1992b. *Homelessness: A Prevention-Oriented Approach.* Baltimore: Johns Hopkins University Press.

Kass, F. I., D. A. Kahn, and A. Felix. 1992. Day Treatment in a Shelter: A Setting for Assessment and Treatment. In *Treating the Homeless Mentally Ill: A Report of the Task Force on the Homeless Mentally Ill,* ed. R. H. Lamb, L. L. Bachrach, and F. I. Kass, 263–277. Washington, D.C.: American Psychiatric Association.

Kauffman, W. 1978. *Critique of Religion and Philosophy.* Princeton, N.J.: Princeton University Press.

Keck, J. 1990. Responding to Consumer Housing Preferences: The Toledo Experience. *Psychosocial Rehabilitation Journal* 13, no. 4 (April), 51–58.

Klein, M. W. 1971. *Street Gangs and Street Workers.* Englewood Cliffs, N.J.: Prentice-Hall.

Koegel, P. 1992. Through a Different Lens: An Anthropological Perspective on the Homeless Mentally Ill. *Culture, Medicine, and Psychiatry* 16, 1–22.

Koegel, P., A. Burnham, and J. Baumohl. 1996. The Causes of Home-lessness. In *Homelessness in America,* ed. J. Baumohl, 24–33. Phoe-nix: Oryx Press.

Koegel, P., A. Burnham, and R. K. Farr. 1990. Subsistence Adaptation among Homeless Adults in the Inner City of Los Angeles. *Journal of Social Issues* 46, no. 4, 83–107.

Kozol, J. 1988. *Rachel and Her Children: Homeless Families in America.* New York: Ballantine Books.

Lamb, R. H., L. L. Bachrach, S. M. Goldfinger, and F. I. Kass. 1992. Summary and Recommendations. In *Treating the Homeless Mentally Ill: A Report of the Task Force on the Homeless Mentally Ill,* ed. R. H. Lamb, L. L. Bachrach, and F. I. Kass, 1–10. Washington, D.C.: American Psychiatric Association.

Lamb, R. H., L. L. Bachrach, and F. I. Kass, eds. 1992. *Treating the Homeless Mentally Ill: A Report of the Task Force on the Homeless Men-tally Ill.* Washington, D.C.: American Psychiatric Association.

Laub, D. N.d. Engaging the Mentally Ill Patient. Manuscript.

Laub, D., and M. Rowe. 1998. Witnessing Homelessness. Manuscript.

Liebow, E. 1993. *Tell Them Who I Am: The Lives of Homeless Women.* New York: Free Press.

Link, B. G., S. Schwartz, R. Moore, J. Phelan, E. Struening, A. Stueve, and M. E. Colton. 1995. Public Knowledge, Attitudes, and Beliefs about Homeless People: Evidence for Compassion Fatigue? *Ameri-can Journal of Community Psychology* 23, no. 4, 533–555.

Lipsky, M. 1980. *Street-Level Bureaucracy: Dilemmas of the Individual in Public Services.* New York: Russell Sage Foundation.

London, J. 1980. *The People of the Abyss.* New York: Joseph Simon.

Lovell, A. M. 1992. Seizing the Moment: Power, Contingency, and Temporality in Street Life. In *The Politics of Time,* ed. H. J. Rutz, American Anthropological Society Monograph Series, no. 4, 86–107. Washington, D.C.: American Anthropological Association.

Lovell, A. M., and S. Cohn. 1998. The Elaboration of "Choice" in a Program for Homeless Persons Labeled Psychiatrically Disabled. *Human Organization* 57, no. 1 (spring), 8–20.

MacBeth, G. 1993. Collaboration Can Be Elusive: Virginia's Experi-ence in Developing an Interagency System of Care. *Administration and Policy in Mental Health* 20, no. 4 (March), 259–281.

Mansouri, L., and D. A. Dowell. 1989. Perceptions of Stigma among the Long-Term Mentally Ill. *Psychosocial Rehabilitation Journal* 13, no. 1 (July), 79–91.

Marin, P. 1987. Helping and Hating the Homeless. *Harper's,* January, 39–49.

Martin, M. 1990. The Homeless Mentally Ill and Community-Based Care: Changing a Mindset. *Community Mental Health Journal 26,* no. 5, 435–447.

McKnight, J. L. 1987. Regenerating Community. *Social Policy,* winter, 54–58.

———. 1992. Redefining Community. *Self-Help and Politics,* fall-winter, 56–62.

Mills, C. W. 1943. The Professional Ideology of Social Pathologists. *American Journal of Sociology* 49, no. 2 (September), 165–180.

———. 1959. *The Sociological Imagination.* New York: Oxford University Press.

Morse, G. A., R. J. Calsyn, J. Miller, P. Rosenberg, L. West, and J. Gilliland. 1996. Outreach to Homeless Mentally Ill People: Conceptual and Clinical Considerations. *Community Mental Health Journal* 32, no. 3 (June), 261–274.

Mossman, D. and M. L. Perlin. 1992. Psychiatry and the Homeless: A Reply to Dr. Lamb. *American Journal of Psychiatry* 149, no. 7 (July), 951–957.

Mullins, S. D., R. Schuh, L. Thomas, K. Thompson, and J. Cyganovich. 1993. *STEPS OUT: A Peer-Integrated Outreach and Treatment Model.* Pittsburgh: n.p.

Oates, J. C. 1986. Introduction. In *Had I a Hundred Months: New and Selected Stories, 1947–1983,* by W. Goyen, vii–xii. New York: Persea Books.

Orwell, G. 1933. *Down and Out in Paris and London.* New York: Harcourt Brace Jovanovich.

Outcasts on Main Street: Report of the Federal Task Force on Homelessness and Severe Mental Illness. 1992. Washington, D.C.: Interagency Council on the Homeless.

Perrow, C. 1986. *Complex Organizations: A Critical Essay.* 3d ed. New York: McGraw-Hill.

Rabinow, P. 1977. *Reflections on Field Work in Morocco.* Berkeley: University of California Press.

Reaching Out: A Guide for Service Providers. 1991. Washington, D.C.: Interagency Council on the Homeless.

Ridgway, P. 1988. *The Voice of Consumers in Mental Health Systems: A Call for Change.* Washington, D.C.: National Institute of Mental Health.

Ridgway, P., A. Simpson, F. Wittman, and G. Wheeler. 1994. Homemaking and Community Building: Notes on Empowerment in Place. *Journal of Mental Health Administration* 21, no. 4, 407–418.

Rosenheck, R., P. Gallup, and L. K. Frisman. 1993. Health Care Utilization Costs after Entry into an Outreach Program for Homeless Mentally Ill Veterans. *Hospital and Community Psychiatry* 44, no. 2 (December), 1166–1171.

Rosenthal, R. 1991. Straighter from the Source: Alternative Methods of Researching Homelessness. *Urban Anthropology* 20, no. 2, 109–126.

———. 1994. *Homeless in Paradise: A Map of the Terrain.* Philadelphia: Temple University Press.

———. 1996. Dilemmas of Local Antihomelessness Movements. In *Homelessness in America,* ed. J. Baumohl, 201–212. Phoenix: Oryx Press.

Rossi, P. H. 1989a. *Down and Out in America: The Origins of Homelessness.* Chicago: University of Chicago Press.

———. 1989b. *Without Shelter: Homelessness in the 1980s.* New York: Priority Press.

Rowe, M., M. A. Hoge, and D. Fisk. 1996a. Critical Issues in Serving Persons Who Are Homeless and Mentally Ill. *Administration and Policy in Mental Health* 23, no. 6 (July), 555–565.

———. 1996b. The Man with the Bright Yellow Sneakers: A Case Example of Assertive Outreach to Mentally Ill Homeless Persons. *Continuum: Developments in Ambulatory Health Care* 3, no. 4 (winter), 265–268.

———. 1996c. Who Cares for Mentally Ill Homeless People?: Individual, Social, and Mental Health System Perspectives. *Continuum: Developments in Ambulatory Health Care* 3, no. 4 (winter), 257–264.

———. 1998. Services for Mentally Ill Homeless Persons: Street-Level Integration. *American Journal of Orthopsychiatry* 68, no. 4, 490–496.

Seeger, C. A. 1990. Reflections on Working with the Homeless. *New Directions for Mental Health Services* 46 (summer), 47–55.

Segal, S. P., and J. Baumohl. 1980. Engaging the Disengaged: Proposals on Madness and Vagrancy. *Social Work* 24, no. 5 (September), 358–365.

———. 1985. The Community Living Room. *Social Case Work: The Journal of Contemporary Social Work* 66, no. 2 (February), 111–116.

Segal, S. P., J. Baumohl, and E. Johnson. 1977. Falling through the Cracks: Mental Disorder and Social Margin in a Young Vagrant Population. *Social Problems* 23, no. 3, 387–400.

Services Integration: A Twenty-Year Retrospective. 1991. Washington, D.C.: Department of Health and Human Services.

Shapiro, J. H. 1971. *Communities of the Alone: Working with Single Room Occupants in the City.* New York: Association Press.

Snow, D. A., and L. Anderson. 1987. Identity Work among the Homeless: The Verbal Construction and Avowal of Personal Identities. *American Journal of Sociology* 92, no. 6 (May), 1336–1371.

————. 1993. *Down on Their Luck: A Study of Homeless Street People.* Berkeley: University of California Press.

Snow, D. A., L. Anderson, T. Quist, and D. Cress. 1996. Material Survival Strategies on the Street: Homeless People as Bricoleurs. In *Homelessness in America,* ed. J. Baumohl, 86–96. Phoenix: Oryx Press.

Snow, D. A., S. G. Baker, L. Anderson, and M. Martin. 1986. The Myth of Pervasive Mental Illness among the Homeless. *Social Problems* 33, no. 5 (June), 407–423.

Spergel, I. A. 1995. *The Youth Gang Problem: A Community Approach.* New York: Oxford University Press.

Spiro, H. M., M. G. M. Curnen, E. Peschel, and D. St. James. 1994. *Empathy and the Practice of Medicine: Beyond Pills and the Scalpel.* New Haven: Yale University Press.

Spradley, J. P. 1970. *You Owe Yourself a Drunk: An Ethnography of Urban Nomads.* Boston: Little, Brown and Company.

Strauss, J. S. 1992. The Person—Key to Understanding Mental Illness: Towards a New Dynamic Psychiatry, III. *British Journal of Psychiatry* 161, supp. 18, 19–26.

Susser, E. S. M. Goldfinger, and A. White. 1990. Some Clinical Approaches to the Homeless Mentally Ill. *Community Mental Health Journal* 25, no. 5, 463–480.

Swayze, F. V. 1992. Clinical Case Management with the Homeless Mentally Ill. In *Treating the Homeless Mentally Ill: A Report of the Task Force on the Homeless Mentally Ill,* ed. R. H. Lamb, L. L. Bachrach, and F. I. Kass, 203–219. Washington, D.C.: American Psychiatric Association.

Swidler, A. 1986. Culture in Action: Symbols and Strategies. *American Sociological Review* 51, 273–286.

Taub, W. K., and L. Sawyers. 1978. *Marxism and the Metropolis: New Perspectives in Urban Political Economy.* New York: Oxford University Press.

Tessler, R., and D. Dennis. 1989. *A Synthesis of NIMH-Funded Research Concerning Persons Who Are Homeless and Mentally Ill.* Rockville, Md.: National Institute of Mental Health.

Townsend, J. M. 1979. Stereotypes of Mental Illness: A Comparison with Ethnic Stereotypes. *Culture, Medicine, and Psychiatry* 3, 205–229.

Vaccaro, J. V., R. P. Liberman, S. Friedlob, and S. Dempsay. 1992. Challenge and Opportunity: Rehabilitating the Homeless Mentally Ill. In *Treating the Homeless Mentally Ill: A Report of the Task Force on the Homeless Mentally Ill,* ed. R. H. Lamb, L. L. Bachrach, and F. I. Kass, 279–297. Washington, D.C.: American Psychiatric Association.

Ware, N. C., R. R. Desjarlais, T. L. Avruskin, J. Breslau, B. J. Good, and S. M. Goldfinger. 1992. Empowerment and the Transition to Housing for Homeless Mentally Ill People: An Anthropological Perspective. *New England Journal of Public Policy* 8, no. 1 (spring–summer), 265–280.

Warren, R. L. 1973. Comprehensive Planning and Coordination: Some Functional Aspects. *Social Problems* 2, no. 3 (winter), 355–364.

Warren, R. L., S. Rose, and A. F. Bergunder. 1974. *The Structure of Urban Reform.* Lexington, Mass: Lexington Books.

Weiss, J. 1981. Substance versus Symbol in Administrative Reform: The Case of Human Services Coordination. *Policy Analysis* 7, no. 2, 21–45.

Wiseman, J. P. 1970. *Stations of the Lost: The Treatment of Skid-Row Alcoholics.* Englewood Cliffs, N.J.: Prentice-Hall.

Wright, J. D. 1988. The Mentally Ill Homeless: What Is Myth and What Is Fact? *Social Problems* 35, no. 2 (April), 182–191.

———. 1990. Poor People, Poor Health: The Health Status of the Homeless. *Journal of Social Issues* 46, no. 4, 49–64.

Yank, G. R., and W. W. Spradin. 1994. Systems Approaches in Mental Health Administration: Linking State and Community Programs. *Administration and Policy in Mental Health* 21, no. 6 (July), 463–477.

Index

ACCESS (Access to Community Care and Effective Services and Supports) project, ix, 14; categorical criteria for clients of, 125; clients of, interviewed for study, x–xi; funding for, 120; ideological framework for, 145; mistrust of, 82–83; patients vs. clients in, 129; quotas in, 127; staff of, interviewed for study, xi–xii

Addams, Jane, 49

Aid to Families with Dependent Children (AFDC), 13

alcohol. *See* substance abuse

Anderson, Leon: "bad luck" theory of homelessness of, 19–20; on homeless identity, 23, 35, 105–106

Assertive Community Treatment (ACT) model, 50

"bad luck" theory of homelessness, 19–20

Barnard, Chester, 41

Baumohl, Jim, 50, 81, 115, 176n54

Baxter, Ellen, 146

Berger, Bennett, 145

border, 1, 156; defined, 2–3; stereotypes associated with, 2

border crossings, defined, 2–3

boundary encounters, 1, 2, 81–119; crisis points in, 89, 159; homeless people's perspective on, 81–89, 157–158; institutional context for, 123–133; nontraditional nature of, 147–148; outreach workers'

perspective on, 81, 89–105, 158; price of accepting help offered in, 105–113; reality vs. appearance in, 115–116; social imagination in, 116–119; structure for, 4–5, 95–105; as test of values of society, 161–162; web metaphor for, 4, 159

Boyer, Paul, 48–49, 79

bureaucracies: as context for boundary encounters, 123–133; improving, 148–151; outreach to homeless and, 120–122; systems integration by, ix, 121–122

categorical funding, 123–128, 130, 158

Chafetz, Linda, 131

citizenship: levels of, 6; program, 146–155; vs. clienthood, 5–6

City Welfare, 25, 39–40

clients: approaching prospective, 63–73, 78–80; on homeless outreach team, 134–137; ideals in working with, 51–52; identification of, 58–63; in partnership with outreach workers, 151–152; price of becoming, 105–113; vs. patients, 129. *See also* homeless people

Cohen, Carl, 151

contingency, 15–20; in approach to prospective clients, 63–64; buffers against homelessness and, 19–20; daily routine filled with, 16;